REMINISCENCES OF
WILLIAM GRAHAM SUMNER

1895

Reminiscences (Mainly Personal)

of

William Graham Sumner

by

A. G. Keller
William Graham Sumner Professor
of the Science of Society
in Yale University

. .
.

. . . That tower of strength
Which stood four-square to all the winds that blew!

New Haven, Yale University Press
LONDON · HUMPHREY MILFORD · OXFORD UNIVERSITY PRESS
1933

William Graham Sumner

UMNER once told me that his *Folkways* was selling beyond his hopes. "It's as good," said he, complacently, "as a bond. I just got sixty dollars from it. More than I ever got from any other book." This was in 1908 or 1909. For a decade or so, *Folkways* was in only moderate demand—a few hundreds of copies a year—though in high esteem among specialists. About 1920, it suddenly began to gain, reaching a record figure of nearly thirteen hundred at its quarter century. Some of us who, also, have watched the term "mores" gradually making an appearance, first in technical literature, then in editorials and articles in newspapers and magazines, and at length in works of fiction, are glad to infer a growing appreciation, outside any special circle, of a great scholar and teacher.

It is not the purpose of the writer of this memoir to deal, except incidentally, with Sumner's scholarship or professional reputation. I strive to follow after that ancient biographer, rather, who sought to record and so to perpetuate the personalities of men whom succeeding generations would do well to remember. The main aspects of Sumner's professional career have been set down with fidelity by Dr. Starr in his *Life of Sumner*. I have deliberately refrained, while jotting down these recollections, from refreshing my memory of that excellent book. I do not intend to write an estimate or critical study of Sumner's work, or even of the man himself. I hold myself under no obligation to weigh pros and cons. I am more interested in the pros, in any case, and shall not be studious to avoid eulogy—though I do not think I shall produce that; for a mighty ghost will stand at my elbow, ready to mutter, in well-remembered tones: "Don't be a gusher!"

I am setting out to record, as they come back to me, my reminiscences—mainly my personal knowledge—of a high-souled man. In the main, I mean to follow the method of Mark Twain in his *Autobiography*—to let the memories come as they will, unarranged, though not, I hope, helter-skelter.

It is my fortune in life to have known Sumner increasingly in-

timately from the fall of 1895 until Christmas Day, 1909, when I
saw him for the last time. As our closer intimacy began when he
was sixty-two and I was twenty-eight, some seven years or so after
I had first entered his undergraduate class, my personal knowledge
of the man is confined mainly to the last seven years of his life. My
relation to him has been, therefore, of the type that may exist between an immature young man and one of his father's contemporaries. What I know of Sumner's earlier years is, except for his
own references to them, either secondhand or inferential.

I have almost no written memoranda to consult. This is a matter
of considerable regret, but it was impossible to improvise a reliable
verbal memory. Close friends used to berate me for not setting
down, at once, the characteristic remarks Sumner used to make
during lengthy walks and talks. Although I tried faithfully, on a
number of occasions, to do so, when I got home I could not remember his exact words; and that was fatal, for the way he put things
was often what made them stand forth as novel and significant. In
fact, if he said merely that it was a fine day, one felt uneasily that
so pregnant an utterance ought to be preserved and reflected upon.
At any rate, I got but little down on paper. There were some of his
sayings, however, that could not be forgotten and even resisted the
tendency to paraphrase; and, in my strivings to secure immunity
from my friends' invectives, I managed to Boswellize a little now
and then.

In the middle nineties, our obscure stage was veritably set for
Sumner's characteristic act of illumination. Three years of college
were behind us, for his course was open to seniors only. I, for one,
had studied a good deal of Latin and Greek; a required minimum
of mathematics; a wretched course in physics; a little dull history;
a couple of years of unproductive drudgery in German; a year of
philosophy which had left me searching myself for the reason why
I had not realized my high hopes in that direction; and several
courses in English. I was one of the many to whom Dr. W. L.
Phelps distributed characteristic nudges toward the cultivation of
a wider acquaintance with English literature. I had been, but was
no longer, worried about religion. However, I was deeply dissatis-
fied, for there seemed to be no convergence about the things I had
faithfully striven to learn. It looked to me, though I had followed, in

the main, a prescribed course of study, as if I had scattered hopelessly and irretrievably. Orderly perspective was lacking, and I felt it, though I did not then know what was the matter. And I was not alone in my discomfort.

With this explanation, or confession, as regards opportunities and inadequacies, I will begin with my first impressions of the man whom I admired from the outset, came shortly to revere, and at length to love.

I

IT can be said that Sumner had a grand start at Yale. The curriculum of the early seventies was pretty dull, unworldly, and lifeless. "He broke upon us," reports a man in the class of 1874, "like a cold spring in the desert." I do not know how many students he had in his classes from 1872 to 1909; the only figures at hand cover the numbers in his one undergraduate course, for seniors only, during the last fifteen years of his service—about three thousand. But they represent only a fraction of his lifetime student following. He had become an institution while he was still young.

I was told, along in my junior year, by some graduate or senior that no one was really entitled to say that he was a Yale B.A. unless he had taken "Billy" Sumner. I had no ideas about who Sumner was or what he taught. I recollect reading the prospectus of his course without enlightenment—a remembrance which has gone far to render me tolerant of what might otherwise have seemed to me, these thirty years, supine obtuseness in the undergraduate. In my case, I signed up for "The Science of Society" on advice and faith, elected to read the German textbook—Sumner ran a team of three, in English, French, and German, respectively—and duly appeared at his first class in the fall. The adventurers upon the German textbook, which was Lippert's *Kulturgeschichte der Menschheit*, were in the first row, close to the high platform, literally—since Sumner sat in a chair near the edge of the platform—at the feet of the master.

I was considerably surprised at the appearance of "Old Bill."

His "magnificent baldness" and "iron voice" have formed the theme of several rhapsodical portrayals. I can say of those attributes that they were thus correctly, if poetically, described. But what struck me was his comparative youth. I had supposed that he was really "old"; he was, as a matter of fact, just fifty-five. There were no signs of decrepitude at all. This is not a retrospective judgment by one who has now surpassed Sumner's age at that time. Very likely he would have looked somewhat older to 1930 eyes than he did to those of the nineties; he had not played golf or tennis like the ancients of today; but he looked young beside his colleagues of equal years and, indeed, beside some of his juniors. Older men who knew the Sumner of the eighties, before his breakdown and two years' absence during his early fifties, say that they came back to be shocked at the change in him; Sumner himself used to complain that he was, after his illness, but half a man; our impression, nevertheless, was not at all that of eld.

At a time when emulation of Homer and Socrates seemed to go with age, Sumner wore no beard. His close-clipped mustache and fringe of hair were not gray; his complexion was ruddy. He looked powerful in body, though his legs seemed to be a little unsteady. He wore no glasses, except that he clapped on a *pince-nez*, rather fiercely, when he had something to read. He was immaculately groomed and clad—a little old-fashioned sometimes, with his tie drawn through a gold band. He told me once that he thought a man should always dress for dinner, but had not himself lived up to that standard. Professor Beers once said that he was the sole instructor, in the sixties, who dressed fastidiously—even a little foppishly—and strode about as if he were a self-respecting man of the world. But he was not vain. He was not at all sensitive about his baldness, but used to speculate as to whether the skin on his head had thickened as a kind of compensatory protection. Once, when we moved offices, I asked him whether a small mirror on the wall was his. "What do I need of a mirror?" he replied, passing his hand over his head.

His movements, in later life, were not quick, but they were firm —in no sense uncertain or feeble. He was slightly bent, but that did not seem to denote weakness. He planted his feet solidly—a little stiff-leggedly and with toes turned out. His feet often hurt him, and once, after he had had them treated, he told me: "I can step out now like a king." When he rode his bicycle, he set the hollow of his foot upon the pedal and seemed to push outward rather than straight down. To some degree he gave the impression of awkwardness, but never of weakness.

In short, there was about him always a dour strength and a scrupulous personal fastidiousness. He generally looked as if he had just emerged from the "bahth," as he called it, and the ministrations of the barber. He was never sloppy in anything—person, clothing, language, or thought.

Except for his face, his most arresting feature was his hand. The fingers were long and bony, and he had a way of enforcing a point by shaking an index-finger which seemed to us from where we sat, almost beneath him, portentously elongated. He was particular about these hands, as I later discovered, and used to trim his nails to an angle. The unexpected about his hand was the lifelessness of his grip; when he greeted you, there was really no clasp at all, for he merely let his hand rest passively in yours for an instant and at once withdrew it. This was probably one of the forms taken by his dislike of contact, but it remained incongruous and disconcerting, even after repeated experience of it.

Sumner's face would have appealed to a Rembrandt. There is said to be in existence a faithful portrait of him. I have never seen it. The most natural photograph of the man in his later years seems to me to be the one in *The Forgotten Man and Other Essays* (p. 92), while the likeness, taken in 1895, that brings him back to me as I first saw him, appears as the frontispiece of *The Challenge of Facts and Other Essays* (frontispiece). It is a little touched up and smoothed out. His eyes were not so open; the pouches beneath them were more accentuated; his face was more furrowed—but it is a grand likeness, none the less. The one in *Earth Hunger and Other Essays* (p. 56) is good and illustrates what has been said about his hands; but it seems to me less characteristic, except that it portrays the milder aspect of the man, about which there is something to record farther on. It is a little artificial, inasmuch, I dare say, as Sumner never felt very complaisant while being photographed. There exists also a snapshot—taken at the time when Sumner, donning his priestly robes, baptized his grandson—that is wholly natural and in particular preserves the look of quizzical tenderness that some of us have seen, especially when he was gazing at a child.

I return to the face, of which, though I am incapable of describing it in competition with these likenesses, there were a few details that the camera could not catch. Sumner's eyes were of a greenish hue—at least they gave that impression. I could not say as to the exact color of the iris. His upper lids were full and heavy, and the pupil appeared to be dilated; it alone seemed visible to one who faced him. The impression it gave was as of the end of an ominous rifle-barrel sticking out of a firing slot. The lower lids also were full and seemed to rise somewhat over the eyeballs. His brows were not marked—there were no pronounced supraorbital ridges—but his eye was piercing. It was not on the order of the "smoldering anthracite furnace," but sharp and cold, and did not seem to participate much in laugh or smile. I do not recall a twinkle, even when he laughed heartily. The students used to say that he looked like an old lion; that was an attempt to describe him in a stern mood. In any case, his eye was a redoubtable and formidable feature, and many there be who have quailed before it.

His nose was long and straight, as the photographs reveal. He used to complain that his teeth were largely metal, but need not have been if it had been the fashion in his youth to care for them. The set of the mouth was stern and resolute. He could look far more disgusted, on occasion, than anyone else I ever saw. I cannot say that his nose turned up at such a juncture, but that was the impression one got. I never saw him angry; disdain always seemed to me to take the place of anger among his facial expressions. He had plenty of practice in expressing detestation, engrossed as he was, all his life, in assaulting men and measures that seemed to him sordid and hall-marked with jobbery. In any case, he had no difficulty in conveying feelings of this order by his facial expression.

WHEN Sumner was serious, he looked stern; and he was almost invariably serious while running his classes. He was, during the time I knew him, almost always physically ailing and not seldom in deep depression about his health, especially when he compared his decreased working-power with the effectiveness of the years of unreasonable tension that preceded his breakdown. He had woes of many kinds that made life look black to him—chiefly, without doubt, the invalidism of his wife. His letters, during her illness, were veritably panicky; one summer, during which he worried sleeplessly over such an illness, he wrote: "All my hopes that we might have a free summer and enjoy life seem to be doomed to disappointment. I cannot work much and if I go out to walk I have the blues so desperately that I dread that too. . . . I have a great deal to go thro before I can see 240 Edwards again. This summer has shortened my life." He did not know how he was going to get his wife home from Seal Harbor and entertained in his desperation the idea of a private railroad car. In the event, the removal was effected with, to him, miraculous ease by use of a litter and the regular small steamers.

Occasionally, too, he rose to a kind of cautious exuberance when all was going pretty well. From Llandudno, Wales, he wrote: "I am rejoicing very much that I feel so well and that my affairs are taking better shape all around and I want every one else to be equally well off." Again: "I shall have two of the loveliest daughters in law on this planet. All my interests prosper. I 'knock on wood' when I say it."

Nevertheless, while I knew Sumner, he went out very little, had small share in the pleasures of life, exercised because his doctor made him do so rather than for the fun of it, and was much alone. He did not whine over his calamities; he brooded. If he was naturally austere and brusque in his external relations, the worries of his latter years of life did little to mitigate that mood. In any case, I am recording the impression of most of his students when I describe Sumner as stern and often forbidding in manner.

It is here that I must set down, at once, that there was another side to this picture which will be much in evidence in later pages. I say, then, that despite all the stories of Sumner's sternness and even coldness—tales circulated by students only half in earnest and greedily caught up by soft-headed, horrified objectors to Sumner's conclusions as to social policies—despite all of this, I aver that no more tender-hearted man has ever come into my range of experience. He had sentiment that was deep and warm, and a sensitiveness that a good woman might well be proud to have ascribed to her. For now I can only say—for I have been talking of Sumner's facial expression—that when that countenance was turned in affection, especially upon a woman or child, it broke up like a shattered pane of glass and beamed—never like a full, fat moon, but the more brightly for the somberness that had cleared away. It was kindliness itself, and mirth too; for, with all his seriousness of outlook on life, Sumner did not lack humor. It broke loose in grim form in the classroom; and it flowed freely in the company of those he cared for most.

BUT I must return to those first days of my acquaintance with the platform figure I have tried to describe. It is no derogation to any of the other professors—now, for the most part, no longer with us—to say that we felt ourselves, many of us for the first time, in a Presence. We came to feel toward him somewhat as Kipling's Norsemen felt toward their leader, who was "red as a red bear," and to his pagans a god; "it was he who cheered them and slew them impartially as he thought best for their needs." His personality was tremendous; still, it could not have held us to loyalty from youth past middle age had it not been accompanied by a knowledge and wisdom which have been verified as we have lived on beyond the range of his eye and voice.

There were almost exactly two hundred of us, out of a class of some two hundred and seventy-five, who gathered that first morning at eight-thirty. Sumner had arrived before us, and at each seat there was a printed sheet, headed "Rules." He began by seating us for the year. We heard the "iron voice" calling our names, and with some concern moved to our designated locations. Sumner came at length to the Smiths, of whom we possessed a generous number, and read off "A. Smith," "N. Smith," and so on down to the last, who happened to have three initials, which Sumner recited with emphasis: "w.D.*G*. Smith!" A suppressed snicker broke out. Sumner hauled off his *pince-nez* and glared a second. "w.D.*G*. Smith!" he repeated, in a tone several registers below his former one, no louder but ominous. Utter silence ensued, while the gentleman named sped rapidly but unobtrusively to his appointed place.

We students stood in awe of the man. He was a disciplinarian beyond compare and tolerated no foolishness. He could handle his large classes, except in his last years, as masterfully as most teachers can manage a tenth of his numbers. But he did not accomplish this by rudeness or terrorism; it was a case of personality plus our conviction that we were getting "the dope."

I have spoken of the list of "Rules." That first morning he began something as follows: "I am no friend of rules." Pregnant pause. "You will find at your places a printed list of rules. They are good ones. I made them myself. You will be held rigidly to them. I will now explain them." There were some dozen or more of these regulations, covering tardiness, manner of handing in the daily ten-minute papers, and so on. His pet aversion was the presence of newspapers in class and, after a few awe-inspiring confiscations, they were kept out of sight. Some of these rules were pretty minute. They were all, Sumner explained, designed to save time and misunderstandings, "so that we shall get along all right together and not waste effort." He was particularly insistent upon having the papers passed in all at once and in a certain order. He did not say why; and he never succeeded in his plan; but it was because, having to read all his tests himself, he begrudged the time required to sort them out alphabetically when it came to entering his grades in the book.

I might add, in this connection, that he had no assistant to read his hundreds of tests until he was well over sixty. He would never ask for one, but plodded desperately through the sordid job, even when ill and faced with the realization that his strength was passing and that he had but a short time left to complete the book of his life. Finally his younger colleagues asked in his behalf for a reader, being careful that he should not know about it; and two hundred dollars were appropriated. He was surprised and told me that the Corporation had opened its heart and voted him money for an assistant—who was J. E. Cutler, now Dean of the School of Applied Social Sciences at Western Reserve. I say that Sumner plowed through these daily tests; but I know of some cases where he piled them into the wastebasket unread, and his old record books show occasional blanks in the grade-columns under certain dates. This was highly exceptional; in the great majority of cases, groaning in spirit and sometimes aloud, he jammed his way through them. The tasks "that I'm paid for" always came first with him, and I think his occasional evasions in the matter of paper-grading preyed not a little upon his conscience.

There is a pronouncement set afloat by wiseacres in the field of education that nothing can be taught through the large lecture course. Nothing can be so taught, doubtless, by the gentry who set up that major premise. Probably they speak out of their own experience; possibly in derogation of the so-called "information courses" of abler men. But Sumner could teach classes of three hundred quite as effectively as many a lesser light could instruct ten, even if the ten *élite* might sip tea and suck churchwarden pipes during the process. As one man put it, he cracked our skulls open with his sledge-hammer blows so that there was room for brain-expansion.

He believed, as he put it, in "keeping school." That meant discipline—indeed, "school-mastering," a term now under contempt. There was a written test—the abhorred ten-minute paper, which is one of the most effective of teaching devices—every day we met. But we felt no grudge against him for his disciplining of us. A great leader can be as severe as he likes—even unjust now and then; and it is imputed to him for virtue or cheerfully borne as one of his characteristic ways, rather amusing than otherwise. Sumner never meant to be unjust, as we well knew. I can still hear him say: "No, 't isn't fair," when some suggestion, say about helping him in some of his routine tasks, was presented to him. No, it was not fear of Sumner that made us hang upon his words. It seems to me that the generations of college men known to me were attracted chiefly by those qualities which I, for one, have so long admired in him: intellectual honesty and fearlessness. Furthermore, young men have always, in my experience, paid tribute to seriousness of purpose, however youthfully wavering they might themselves have been; "Bill," we said, "means business." And they have made obeisance to knowledge that has seemed to them worth having, or that some great teacher has caused them to value. There is no possible doubt, either, that they love the dramatic, though I think they quickly tire of the merely spectacular. And they deeply appreciate genuine humor—in fact, I think that a sense of humor is an indispensable for distinguished teaching.

Now Sumner had all these qualities in high degree. We were

serenely and unshakenly convinced that he believed what he said, and said what he thought without paying the slightest attention to what people might say. Particularly were we subtly influenced by having no concessions made to our verdancy or tender years. We knew that we got from Sumner just what grown men would get. He spoke to us as man to men. He granted us minds and character, and appealed directly to them, but with no claims to any mere reverence for his authority. He taught us to stand on our own legs and face issues without dodging or flinching.

SOME have said that Sumner's clarity was due to the fact that he never saw but one side to a question, and therefore was not bothered by the need of hedging and shading. It certainly conduces to clarity to see an issue in that way; but it would not be fair to one who has stood to so many as a champion and exponent of fairness to let this offhand version go unchallenged. The Commencement orator of 1909, when Sumner received the Yale doctorate of laws, said: "Like all great teachers and real leaders of men, he is intensely dogmatic; but his dogmas are not the result of narrowness or prejudice; they come from prolonged study and profound thought." This sentence contains, implicitly at least, the *rationale* of Sumner's dogmatism. He was always teaching the elements of social science to beginners, whether they sat in his classes or not; and in the teaching of the elements dogmatism is necessary. Any teacher who knows his business is aware that some well-defined standpoint must be gained before the balancing of theories can be profitably begun. Hence Sumner was, in his teaching and essays, very positive; and the worth of this pedagogical device is vouched for by many—even by those who now dispute the positions upheld by Sumner. I do not mean to say that Sumner did not thoroughly believe in what he said; he was intellectually honest to the extent of refusing to support in debate the easier, more plausible, but to him the wrong side of a question. His flatly stated opinions were the result of long study; what he presented was the building without the scaffolding. This could readily be seen by his more advanced students, for in his graduate classes he opened up to us his doubts and perplexities in the frankest manner; and no one could talk with him as man to man without becoming aware that he held all his scientific opinions open to revision. His mind was essentially hospitable to new truth; but pending its emergence he clung with great loyalty to what he regarded as already demonstrated. Above all, he clave to "common sense," and used often to urge us to hold in abeyance any theory which seemed to conflict with it; for correspondence with common sense was, to him, an ultimate test.

Sumner's attitude toward his profession was marked by a certain austerity. He would sometimes regret that he had not gone into law, but was never apologetic as respects his profession, though he used in private to joke about it in a grim sort of way. This quality of austerity was especially happy in a man who stood for sociology; for if any modern science needs the austere exponent, it is precisely that one. "The field of sociology," Sumner once said to me, "is so raw that any crank can fasten on it from any angle." Here was an apt arena for a man whose grand message to his students was, as one of them crystallized it: Don't be a damn fool! He had no use for the sensationalist or the man with the program, and it was partly for this reason that he paid so little attention to "practical sociology" and reiterated in his lectures and in the announcements of his courses that the science of society as he taught it was based upon the facts of ethnography and history. He had comparatively little faith in systematic works on sociology and paid but slight attention to them; if I take his attitude rightly, it was not that of "intellectual arrogance," as some have asserted, but resulted from the belief that extended theorizing and ambitious attempts at systematization are not suited to the early phases of a new science. There is too much else to do.

What matter, then, if Sumner was dogmatic? There must be something solid to set foot upon, and I do not know what could be better adapted to the purpose than the matured conclusions, drawn from long and intimate acquaintance with the facts, of a mind whose single interest is the truth. What matter if later study and experience cause you to question such conclusions? You have, at least, something positive to correct or reject; and are challenged by your very respect for what you have been strongly taught not to abandon it for less than serious reason.

I believe, indeed, that many a man has been goaded to study things out for himself for very rage at the conclusive manner in which Sumner disposed of some of his pet or traditional notions. Sometimes such a man came to agree with Sumner; again he believed that he had won the right not to assent—but in either case there had come to him an awakening in the matter of his own mental powers and life. This is why so many men who have eventually come to dissent from Sumner's positions, yet look back upon him as an intellectual awakener. The difficult thing about getting a vision in the large is in the attainment of an elevated plane of thought; if someone can lift you to it, you will find room enough there to range away from the exact spot upon which you were originally set down. It is the "lift" which is crucial—and that it is which only the strong and positive man, who has wrought himself up beyond the pull of the trivial and traditional, can give.

IT has been said that Sumner had matter, manner, and method —all three, but that the greatest of these was manner. Some have thought that his whole secret lay in his manner. There is no doubt that he was a striking personality. He spoke with impressive conviction and generally with impressive pauses. His face, his voice, his figure, his hands—all these contributed to the effect he got, and perhaps deliberately sought. He had a way of prolonging or drawling long words, such as "societology" (só-ci-et-ól-o-gée—he avoided the term "sociology" because of its "soft-headedness") which in a lesser man might have seemed laughable, instead of interestingly odd. We never laughed at such peculiarities, for to us, when he was speaking, it seemed that we were in the range of large and vital issues. He had an affection for certain pronunciations (such as "Chaldaea," the first two letters as in "chair") and stuck to them, it seemed, merely because he wanted to. "It don't" was common enough in his discourse: "It don't pay to whine." Words of German origin he generally refused to anglicize, and cross-references in his notes were often in German: "See Evil Eye, *nebenbei*." Measurements upon the skull, the use of salt, clay tablets—such matters took on, under his intent seriousness, a deep significance. Once he lectured for several hours, all told, on the coin shilling of Massachusetts Bay; and we all, though graduate students then, took down his elaborate calculations from the blackboard as if they were gospel—indeed, many of us felt that we should somehow fall short if we did not sometime own a piece-of-eight.

I think I should try to reproduce Sumner's illustration of "antagonistic coöperation," as I can recall it. "Down in Africa, the hippopotamús comes up out of the mud, all—covered—with—slugs. They stick to his ears, and nose, and eyelids. Then comes along the tick-bird and picks them off. He can see first rate, but the hippopotamús can't, and his twitterings warn the hippopotamús of danger, while he gets his pay by feeding on the slugs. Does the tick-bird love the hippopotamús? No! Does the hippopotamús love the tick-bird? No! Case of antagonistic coöperation."

One who reads over his old notebook on the Science of Society course sometimes cannot see just why the course laid hold of him so strongly; but then he closes his eyes and recalls the manner of presentation—the authority of a face whose very ruggedness was not a matter of lines without, but rather of straightness, of undeviating and uncompromising honesty and sincerity, within—and the spirit reënters the dull and boyish pencilings, and all is explained. That was why he compelled us to think, to accept or to resist, it mattered not which; no "copious shuffler," no half-scholar, no shirk or mere pleasure-lover, no man who had not grappled with the grimnesses of thought, could thus, apparently without conscious effort, have compelled our intellectual homage. One reflects upon his old notebook again and presently he sees that there was yet something more in the case—call it method, if one will, it was yet a living demonstration of the method being the man—and that was the simplicity always characteristic of Sumner and his work. No long words where a short one could be found, and no wastefulness even of the monosyllables; crisp, curt sentences as devoid as possible of latinity; no ideas so lofty and tenuous as to be incapable of full comprehension by the normal, healthy, youthful mind. The intellectual draught he reached us was so clear in its quality that sometimes, in retrospect, it looks as if there were nothing there at all. The ideas in the old notes seem so familiar as to be almost axiomatic; and yet, if we reflect upon them, we realize that they came to us first from Sumner and that they are in our notes because we hurried to get them down as being so new and grand to our youthful minds. Now they are part of us; for

Sumner is living in us all and in those whom we shall have influenced, as he is living in the college in whose service he found no labor too great—nor yet too small. He disciplined us and chastised us, and we return thanks for it; he opened our minds, taught us to detect and hate humbug, to trust to the truth, and to be faithful to duty—and for that we tender him our enduring reverence. The simple fidelity of a powerful man is an abiding treasure of remembrance, and a bracing one.

Perhaps the most impressive thing about the man was that one straightway forgot his intellect and work when one was led to contemplate the union of austerity and tenderness which made up his character. If he has any enemies now living, I am sure they would all agree that, for a mortal man, Sumner had about him nothing that was *small*. To those who knew him well, it seemed that he must possess an almost intuitive sense of rectitude; for as his unrivaled mental acumen and common sense were wont to pierce so keenly the husks that surrounded any intellectual issue and to adjudge it according to its merits in its more than local setting, in like manner did his delicate sensitiveness to the quality of a moral issue serve as a sort of touchstone for those privileged to know him well. Nothing mean or low could thrive in his presence. But the steel of his character was not so delicate as to snap or to lose its cutting edge in the rudest of combats; he was "great in war." Sensitive of soul and strong of heart, his voice was one "from which their omens all men drew."

Some years ago, Mr. Henry Holt asked me to write him something that would do for publicity in connection with Dr. Starr's *Life of Sumner*. I do not know that I can do better than to reproduce part of what I then wrote, for I made a serious effort to recall our attitude of curiosity concerning Sumner's past.

Along with many other men of my time, I regarded Sumner as the champion mind-opener. Entrance into his classes offered a novel vision of knowledge in broad perspectives. His scope was so great that everything I had learned previously seemed, under his influence, to drop into its proper place and assume utility for the understanding of life. In short, along with many others of my time, I regarded Sumner as a great intellectual liberator.

Before I came personally to know him—and this was the case with a number of others—I was immensely curious as to what sort of a man he was, and in particular how he had arrived at the power which he showed. As we saw him, he seemed like a mighty, self-contained, finished product of nature, like a glacier or a volcano. He was the despair of all of us because of the gigantic industry and power which he exhibited. We were all curious to know what he had been before he arrived where he was. We had also heard that he was originally a clergyman and that stimulated our curiosity very greatly because we could not reconcile his views with what we then knew as ecclesiastical positions.

I will say that if a life of Sumner had at that time been available, we should have pounced upon it as eagerly as upon the stray bits concerning his past which somehow drifted to us. Some of this information was so evidently apocryphal that even we were incredulous concerning the truth of it. I suppose there are a good many men of all ages who have had this curiosity about Sumner, and who do not to this day know anything about his previous life and concerning the forces which conspired to make him what he was.

THERE is no question that Sumner cast a kind of spell over his hearers; but it was not all, or nearly all, referable to manner and sheer personality. There was plenty of matter—so much, indeed, that the listener constantly marveled at the industry revealed in the scope of knowledge he exhibited. Then some of us were taken up into the third-floor study of his home and shown the thousands of notes and excerpts from his colossal reading, standing in close and serried ranks in box after box, drawer after drawer. When he had laid down his life-work, his materials were found to fill fifty-two receptacles, each of which, by rough calculation, contained some three thousand filed and classified notes, covering readings from books and journals in over a dozen languages. Such persistent industry could not but show through, even through elementary lectures, so as to impress immature young men with confidence in the competence of their instructor. Later, we found that Sumner had done all this work by himself; he did not pilfer; he was not a hero of padded bibliographies, allusive trappings, or composite research. Of this more, later on.

Besides manner, then, Sumner had voluminous matter over which he had pondered through hours of that solitude in which, says

Goethe, talent comes to its development. The essence of his method was its simplicity, for it was compounded of only two prime elements: industry and common sense. For the tenuous refinements of "methodology," Sumner had only ridicule. "The way to do it is to use common sense; you start off and go right along," was about all he would say on that score. Upon a certain occasion, he was invited to address a convention of school teachers. He at first refused but later reconsidered, remarking that he had, after all, something he would like to say to them. His address was brief and consisted chiefly of a story or parable. The convention was devoting itself largely to questions of methodology, under the guidance of pedagogical seers. Sumner's story was something as follows.

"When I was in college, I knew a fellow who got all worked up over *how* to study. He had lots of theories. He tried it sitting down, lying down, standing up, standing on one leg, and so on. When the examination came, he flunked and was dropped from college. He hadn't studied at all. He had spent his time getting ready to do something. He didn't know anything."

With this may be compared Sumner's terse prescription for learning to read a foreign language: "The way to learn a language is to sit down and learn it."

Undergraduate students know little about formal method, and care less. They like results. What they unconsciously imbibe out of their environment, however, from tender years, is deduction—always deduction. They are not taught much about causes—impersonal causation; but ever, as accounting for all things, is personal agency set before them, chiefly in the guise of the Great Man, the hero to worship. Generations have had to cram Carlyle's *Heroes and Hero Worship* rhapsody for entrance to college. No wonder that *foie gras* results. They are fed upon grand, shaky major premises and imposing visions of idealized lives of great men, of footprints on the sands of time, and of other edifying and ethical mythology. Through such *a priori* constructions Sumner drove a mighty battering-ram that left much wreckage. "Always," he enjoined upon us, "*dig out the major premise;* you can get out of a major premise just what is put into it—no more and no less. If it's grand enough, like 'All men are created free and equal,' you can get anything out of it, and all false." Of course there was lamentation and resistance as the pieces flew before his assault; but young men are far from being supine fools and, besides, they are not averse to a Roman holiday; and many of them followed Sumner joyously through the breach he had ripped and came out into a freer air on the far side. Having thus emerged, they conceived a profound respect for the sort of conditioning that had made Sumner's intellectual charge so shattering. They learned to appreciate, even if they could not follow his example, the value of hard, sustained intellectual strain coupled with a passion for seeing the facts of life as they are and a courage to go along with cautious and honest conclusions as far as they might lead.

In general, Sumner strove to be a scientist, taking science to be no more than "trained and organized common sense." When he had caught the scientific point of view, he became a militant apostate from his early training in metaphysics and theology. "I've been heaving that cargo overboard ever since," he told me. "Metaphysics," he writes, "has never done anything for me but weight me down. I took to it zealously when a young man and have been fighting it ever since, to try to free my mind from its influence. However, *metaphysics rules the civilized world today.*" Again: "Keep cool and damn all metaphysics." But I think the effort to jettison never arrived with him at a complete riddance of a lading once eagerly stowed. Fragments of the viscous stuff still stuck here and there. Indeed, he himself used to bewail the fact. Sumner's whole heart was set upon "getting at the facts," and the spirit of his strivings, despite any and all handicaps due to his early training, passed over to those who came to look confidently, if uncritically, to him for trustworthy guidance. At the very least, it rendered many men, in later life, wary of the products of introspection, meditation, and speculation. It made strongly against credulity and acquiescence in nose-leading. "But," many a man has said to others, or to himself, as he has faced some muddled or equivocal issue, "as Old Billy used to say, . . ."

By whatever means, Sumner taught intellectual honesty and independence, thus building, as I have contended, upon generous tendencies already pronounced, or latent and evokable, in young manhood. And not the least compelling of the factors in his equipment was his willingness to abandon at once any position that was shown not to square with the facts. Naturally this trait came out less clearly in his elementary classes, but it emerged often enough to reinforce with power our belief that he cared only for the truth. On one occasion, a student held up his hand during the lecture. Sumner paused: "Well?"

The student: "I have been studying up the subject you are treating, and I do not agree with you."

Sumner: "That is your right."

We never suspected him of twisting or evading or "interpreting." His waspish sallies before tariff commissioners delighted us. We believed that he dared face anything. To us he was suspicion-proof.

I think it is evident enough that Sumner was dramatic. But it was always a dignified and even austere drama that he enacted. He was never a showman. He was never sensational; neither he nor his successors have aimed at or attained notoriety, for themselves or their university, by incontinent and startling rushes into the lime-light. He conceived of teaching as a serious and weighty business. His eye was always on what he was trying to say—not on his audience and how they might feel about it—not on himself, still less on the manner of the saying. For manner without matter he had only contempt. Verbal sleight-of-hand disgusted him. He told me that he had listened once to a certain "glib" lecturer with a wide reputation and had been impressed by him. "But as I walked home, I asked myself just what he had said, and I found that he hadn't said anything at all. He'd just made a seductive noise. *Lauter Windbeutel!* And then I didn't go to hear him any more." With Sumner, impressiveness of presentation came almost solely out of depth of conviction. I do not recall that he told a single story in his classes. He never tried to raise a laugh. He never made concessions to the youth and flightiness of his students. His touch was never light nor were there any decorations—what he called "frills"—to his exposition. It was plain, hard, and ruthless. It was as implacable, uncompromising, and challenging as the roar of a lion. In it were no amenities at all.

But he was as fastidious in his diction as he was in his person. There was nothing cheap about it—never a preciosity, no pose. There was no filigree-work, nothing artfully elaborated. It was granitic—not elegant, not beautiful, not "cultured" in the narrow sense but graphic in the manner of Aeschylos and other such serious souls who, in the effort to transmit massive ideas, have borne forth newly quarried and still jagged blocks rather than polished fragments. "The way to raise wages is to work, not to not work."

THIS does not mean that Sumner was careless of his English, or raw in style. His blue-pencilings of doctoral dissertations were devastating to the meticulous typing which, we candidates hoped, would make its modest appeal. In his lectures he used slang as little as he employed decorative allusion. And, though his distaste for Johnsonian latinity and his love for terse Anglo-Saxon words and short sentences came, in his last years, to approach mannerism, he spoke, as he wrote, clearly, forcefully, and with an unobtrusive background of discriminating taste formed upon a wide acquaintance with the best literature of the ages.

It should not be forgotten that he was familiar—and in the original—with the authors who wrote Job and the Odyssey, with Vergil, Dante, Goethe, Ibsen, Strindberg, Dostoyevsky, Sienkiewicz, Calderón, Molière, Camoens. There was doubt, in 1871, whether he would be called to Yale as professor of Greek or of Political Science. At one time in his early life he thought of becoming a poet. Such scope has its reflection in style as well as content; there were in Sumner's discourses a good many subtle appeals to young men of divers antecedents and tastes. He got at the spirit of what he read and studied, and the composite of genuine culture was unmistakable.

I say that Sumner made us no jokes and told us no stories—not stories as such, though there were pregnant parables. There were flights of fancy, always to the point; consider the passage in *Protectionism, the -Ism which teaches that Waste makes Wealth*, where the author impatiently breaks into dialogue between the discoverer of an iron deposit and his Congressman. It tempts to quotation but is too long and cannot be condensed.

Here are a few samples of Sumnerisms; a large collection could be made, especially from his essays. "It's the same force that makes the stone go down and the balloon go up." "If you ever live in a [Communist] country run by a Committee, *be on the Com-*

mittee." "When people cry out virtuously against jobbery, it may be because they are virtuous, or it may be because they are sorry they are not in the steal." "These Dutchmen of the East India Company, and a good many of our Pilgrim Fathers, prayed a lot and stole themselves rich." "In the Colonies, during inflation, you might see creditors fleeing madly from debtors who were chasing them to pay them with bushel-basketfulls of dirty paper." "There was once a man who gave out that he meant to be all things to all men. It is not related that he succeeded." Of Andrew Jackson: "In his last years he joined the church, and, on that occasion, under the exhortations of his spiritual adviser, he professed to forgive all his enemies in a body. . . . It does not appear that he ever repented of anything, ever thought that he had been in the wrong in anything, or ever forgave an enemy as a specific individual."

This was the type of Sumner's humor: grim, mordant, ironical. There was also a spice of stinging satire. But it was funny, the more so as it came without announcement, overture, or hint. The effect was that of pure spontaneity. Sumner never smiled, or only faintly, as he struck off some grotesque "dig"; he waited a moment while we laughed and then hurried back to seriousness as if a little ashamed, though I think he was not.

This humor of his, keen and often flashing, endeared him to young men as only that quality can. It lent interest. It might come any time, unannounced; and when it did, one wanted to get it. Its rarity enhanced its quality. Here was another case of "In der Beschränkung zeiget sich der Meister." Furthermore, since Sumner's thrusts were not premeditated but evoked by the occasion, they were almost always new and sharply milled—directly from the mint. Such fresh coin is attractive, and it is a little flattering to feel that an issue has been run off for one's own special sake. Sumner's coin was never tarnished by antecedent handling or blurred by some sweating process. He did not repeat himself. He didn't need to.

I suppose that nothing else in a teacher strikes classes of young men as feebler and more craven than an attempt to placate or conciliate them. It is, to their eyes, a form of dodging and even of cowardice. Sumner was no more conciliatory than a top-sergeant. On the other hand, his satire was never directed toward his students—something that strikes young men as eminently unfair and unsportsmanlike. Nor could he be hoodwinked. On one occasion, it is reported, a certain hardy youth proposed that they try to get Sumner involved in some discussion, at the beginning of the hour, so that he would forget to give his regular ten-minute test. This sort of enterprise had repeatedly succeeded with another professor. The youth's comrades, though highly dubious about trying it on Sumner, were quite willing that the proponent should make the attempt if he dared. He did. He primed himself upon some economic issue then under discussion and, just as Sumner was about to give out his question, raised his hand. "Well?" growled Sumner. The young man asked his question and to the delighted amazement of the class Sumner spent the whole period in discussing it.

At the end of the hour, he stopped and eyed his questioner in silence for a moment. "I'm glad you brought up that point," he remarked. "I might not have thought to do it myself." Pause; then very grimly: "*I—know—why* you did it." Longer pause; then, with a wintry smile: "Double paper next time."

An incident alluded to by Dr. Starr illustrates most vividly Sumner's relations of utter candor with his classes. The year in question he had had an extraordinarily large enrollment and—it was shortly before he retired—had not been able to control the class as he always had done before. There had been, off and on, some noise and inattention that had irked him sore. Toward the end of the year either the disorderly had repented of their discourtesy or else feared reprisals; in any case, there was bought for Sumner a large, silver loving-cup, and a certain eminent senior, captain of one of the teams, was deputed to present it at the opening of the hour. He strode up the aisle, his trepidation increasing as he approached the formidable presence—for Sumner did not look pleased at all. The transporter of the precious vessel said afterward that he wished he had had a stick "to poke it over to him with."

Sumner took the cup and set it down on the table beside him. Then he looked over the class in silence, and without exhibiting any pleasurable emotion whatever. At length he spoke. "I'm not accustomed to make valedictories, but one seems to be called for this time." He stopped, leaned forward, and spoke with restrained emphasis. "I've—been—counting—the hours till I got rid of you!"

He paused to let that sink in; then castigated the class, in chosen words, for their disrespect and ill conduct in general. His analysis, said one of them, was thorough and pungent. After thus discharging his obligation to speak the truth, he stopped, looked at the cup, smiled grimly, and concluded: "But perhaps this indicates a better disposition: and I will say this: I will try to think as well of you as I can, for the rest of my life." Slight pause. "The question for the day is as follows: . . ."

Now, no one took this plain speaking amiss. It was "Old Bill's way"; also he had good reason. I am informed that he was secretly much pleased and exhibited the cup at home with the remark: "See what the boys gave me today. Very polite of them."

Perhaps I may add a companion-piece out of personal experience, illustrative of Sumner's habit of speaking out the truth as a basis of understanding. Early in my relations with him, he was somewhat offish and disapproving. He had warned me against taking on certain obligations before I was more stable upon my financial feet, and I had disregarded the advice. He was pretty distant with me until, one Sunday afternoon, he met me on the street accompanied by a member of the family, aged two. He thawed out at once. "So this is the baby!" he exclaimed, and held out a long forefinger to her, which she grasped without hesitation. He stopped to talk with her, paying no attention to me. A few drops of rain fell. He turned to me sternly: "Take that child home at once; it's beginning to rain." He seemed thereafter to feel that I had somehow justified my existence.

A few days later, he stopped me. "Keller," he said, "we have been wanting to have you and Mrs. Keller to dinner, but Mrs. Sumner has been ill and away at a sanatorium and, since she got home, she has not been able to go out at all or to receive much of any. She has been unable to call upon Mrs. Keller, and isn't up to it now. I shall do myself the honor to call in her place, and then we want you, and the baby, to dine with us."

When I reported the situation at home, Mrs. Keller, who had a rather vivid impression of Sumner as an implacable taskmaster to me, was not a little concerned over the impending ordeal. Several days later, when I got home, I was informed that Mr. Sumner had been and gone. I saw at once that he had left no trail of devastation. Mrs. Keller had entered rather timidly the room where he was waiting. He rose and smiled ingratiatingly. "I am Mr. Sumner," he stated, and immediately came out with: "I guess I had better tell you right off, and have it done with, that I—opposed—your—marriage." He paused to let his culpability sink in, then: "I thought Keller was crazy. But I want to say now that everything seems to have come out all right. You're getting along, and you have a beautiful baby. Now, Mrs. Sumner couldn't call on you, but if I will do . . ." and so on with his message.

Even in the smallest things, he was absurdly honest. Once he invited us, on certain conditions, to visit him during the summer: "You see that I have dealt with you openly and told you just how things are. I wanted very much to get you all here but I have not humbugged you any. We will try again next summer."

As a host, Sumner was ideal. His solicitude for the comfort of his guests was comprehensive. When we were to visit him at Fisher's Island we always received full and minute directions concerning trains and ferries, with cautions as to this and that possibility of going astray; and when we had arrived, were taken into the family in the most charming fashion. Sumner did not talk shop, nor did he pose in any way; he was easy in manner and interested in what his guests had to say. Especially was he deferential to opinions offered by them, even when, as I knew, he held opposite views. While he was entertaining, there was, as it were, a closed session upon debate. He would occasionally poke gentle fun at some of the views expressed by the ladies. In any case, he set his guests promptly at their ease, never thinking of himself at all, and solicitously and tactfully served them at all times and in all ways.

PERHAPS I have rambled on far enough with reflections on Sumner as an undergraduate teacher. We parted with him about the first of June, 1896. When we came in that last time, the extensive blackboard was completely covered with his writing. I do not recall that it was referred to much in his lecture that day. At the end of the hour we clapped a long time, then cheered and applauded for a good many minutes. Sumner did not bow or otherwise pay attention to our demonstration, but hastened to the board and began, with his back to us, to erase what was upon it. As we stayed on in our seats, applauding, he erased more and more slowly, evidently to make the task last out until we should have gone and he could turn about. My impression is that he was much flushed, clear to the back of his head. He made the bogus task last out; then we went outside and cheered him lustily on the steps. I suppose he found the ordeal highly embarrassing and would gladly have eluded all the manifestations of our approval. Still, I think he appreciated his popularity too. He could not have failed to see the wholeheartedness of our sentiments, and he was himself, at bottom, very sentimental.

I have elsewhere intimated that Sumner's work, especially in his latter phase, was but little appreciated by some who should have known better, even by colleagues who professed to admire his earlier accomplishments. But this does not refer to his under-graduate and graduate students. In 1907 he was recommended by some of us for the doctorate of laws, but we were told that prece-dent was against a university thus honoring its own men. The next year, when we nominated him again, I was informed that since Sumner was an individualist and the present age one of altruism, his nomination was not likely to be popular. However, he was given the LL.D. on his retirement, in June, 1909, and the ovation he received, one of the University officers who had been dubious told me, surpassed anything of the kind that he had ever seen. I have a long descriptive letter from a classmate who witnessed it. Fathers and sons got up and roared their applause when Sumner rose, when he received his diploma and hood, and again when he retired to his seat. They kept him standing for several moments at each out-burst. Sumner told me that the cheering took him completely by surprise and overwhelmed him. "I thought my legs wouldn't hold me up to get to my seat, and my eyes were full of tears so I couldn't see where I was going." In a brief autobiographical note, he writes: "My relations with students and graduates have always been of the pleasantest, and I think that there can be but few rela-tions in life which can give greater satisfaction than these." This, his estimate of the compensations of his university connection, represents the drift of his conversational allusions to it. There are significant omissions in his statement. Some other aspects of his profession irritated him deeply. One day Sumner burst out that he would resign at once if he could afford to. "You couldn't bear to," I replied. He pulled out his watch. "It is now ten-fifteen," he said; "if I could afford it, my resignation would be in by noon."

What Yale men think of him and his service to them is strikingly shown by the formation, several years after his death, of the Sumner Club, an organization of younger and older Yale graduates, and including also some non-Yale admirers, among them the much-mourned Dwight Morrow. The main object of this organization, which has grown and thriven year by year, was to assist Sumner's successor and legatee in completing *The Science of Society*. That successor at first refused the aid proffered, fearing the protraction of the task before him; but the men who had the enterprise at heart argued that he had no right to exclude them from participation in supporting their faith in "Sumnerology," and he must needs yield. No more magnanimous and loyal intellectual enterprise is known to me. When I survey evidence of this sort as to the influence of Sumner, not to mention his other eminent services to his generation, I can scarcely believe that any Yale man could have expressed surprise, when Dr. Starr's *Life of Sumner* came out, that Sumner should have been deemed of sufficient moment to deserve a biography.

During the summer of 1909, after his retirement and the conferring upon him of the doctorate of laws, I was with him for a time at Fisher's Island. Every morning we used to call at the local post office as we started on a walk toward one of the promontories overlooking the Sound. As we went on, he would open his letters. One day he passed a sheet over to me. "Like to look at this?" he suggested. It was an appreciative and affectionate tribute from a student who had been in his classes several years before, its occasion being his retirement and academic honors. "That's a fine thing," said I. "I know the man and it is exactly what he thinks. You ought to feel pretty well satisfied to get such letters." "I've had a lot of 'em this summer," he grunted. "Yes, the world's using me pretty well nowadays." And he at once changed the subject. But he was quite cheerful, those days, especially after the morning mail, and, when we had climbed the hill and sat or lay on the grass in the sun, related a series of incidents, both grave and gay, out of his life. Would that I could have registered them in his own words!

II

IN his dealings with his classes of graduate students, Sumner seemed to act upon some private variant of the theory about the survival of the fittest. Having picked up your heels and tipped you overboard head first, he seemed to take no further interest in your fate, but rowed off on his own business. I judge that he expected you to swim out by yourself or else to go under— either alternative representing a kind of natural selection. Of all things, he hated "whining" and seemed to like a man the better for not taking chastisement, including that which he himself dispensed, "lying down." He gave out, in October, a formidable list of books upon which he stated that he would set an examination in June. There were no conferences and if, as only occasionally happened, a member of the class read a prepared paper, there were few or no comments. If you sought an interview, he would briefly reply to what definite questions you might ask, but that was all. I think this was a procedure, or lack of it, dictated by conviction—certainly not by laziness, though doubtless, in his preoccupation with time-saving, he was impatient of distraction.

From time to time he was much bored by earnest souls in his classes, such as the one who came to him with the subject of his doctor's thesis already selected: "The Relation of God to the Universe." This man pestered Sumner with metaphysical queries. "I couldn't stand it any longer," Sumner told me, "so I said: 'Don't come to me with any more of these questions. Study the books I assigned, and you will either discover the answers to your questions or find out how foolish they are.'" The person in question ended up with a fine doctor's dissertation on the local industry of a small manufacturing town.

Casually enough, Sumner would set formidable tasks, drawing large sight-drafts on one's time and industry. "Get Italian this summer," he commanded tersely, when one of us sought advice as to the first graduate year. The following June he inquired: "Did you get Italian last summer? Well, then, Dutch and Danish this time." And, once again, the next year: "Spanish and Portuguese now." It was not that he thought these tasks easy; he said that he was not quick at getting languages. I noticed later, in his grammars and lexicons, evidence that he "crammed up the paradigms," as he called it, like any beginning student. In learning Swedish, for instance, he followed his manual faithfully, translating not only all the Swedish-English exercises but the English-Swedish. Sheets of paper have turned up upon which he had written and rewritten the Spanish verbs. I have been told that learning Russian was the last straw, or beam, that broke him down, and that he had followed about the most bungling grammar—a Russian-German one—that he could have found.

When he set such tasks, he expected that they would be performed as he had performed them, and was immensely disgusted with short cuts. "You haven't crammed up the declensions and conjugations? Then you don't know the thing and can't read it!" If one of us suggested that he could read one of these languages well enough to get all he needed for his professional purposes, Sumner would snort impatiently: "It's no way to do it!" He himself could read such literature as *Peer Gynt*, where we had been content to spell our way through easy prose. One summer he wrote me that he wasn't doing much: "I am now half thro *With Fire and Sword* in the original. It begins to slip along fairly well. I never got Polish so as to read at sight. I hope now to do it." Having covered the four-volume trilogy of Henryk Sienkiewicz, he seemed, in the fall, to feel a higher self-respect. With such exploits are to be aligned his review of his college mathematics and his acquisition of calculus, in order that he might see for himself what there was in mathematical economics. He was probably led to his Russian by a strong curiosity concerning the real nature of the village community, the *mir*. In the cases of the mathematics and the Russian, he told me, the results had not been worth the effort.

This insistence upon language was to him as reasonable as the requirement that an apprentice in a trade should know his tools. And his matter-of-fact prescription, quoted above, jolted some of his students out of their sacred terror of a foreign tongue. "The way to learn a language," he used to say, "is to sit down and learn it. I'll lend you a grammar and a dictionary." As for himself, we found, he had emulated the Catos and the Huxleys by acquiring the languages he read—other than Hebrew, Greek, Latin, French, and German—probably all after the age of forty-five.

It may be interpolated here that, while he lent us his old books freely, he hated to lend several costly ones, sumptuously printed and bound, which he had come to own. He would pick up a volume of his Maspero, *Histoire Ancienne*, for instance, look at it doubtfully, then say: "I don't want to lend this; I guess you will have to use the Library copy."

Perhaps we had better have been studying something else than language. I am not sure. But Sumner's large assumption of what we could do, plus our awe at his own amazing example of industry, was certainly a considerable factor in our education under him. It was one of the ways in which he created an atmosphere, the more impressive in that we had grown up in a monolingual environment and had been taught modern language as if it were ancient and dead.

H AVING strapped upon our backs such loads as he thought expedient, Sumner, for the rest, proceeded to introduce us into what might be called his "shop." He would bring in a sizable block of his notes, impart by lecture their content to us, and show us what he was doing with them—what could be got out of them. It was precisely what he was doing, or intended to do, in the making of a science of society. It was case-teaching, a plain demonstration of genuine induction. Though he could not bring in all his data, he gave us the distinct impression that whatever generalizations he arrived at took their origin in the cases, and not otherwise. He made it clear to us that, on what evidence he had—and he meant to assemble a great deal more—an issue looked thus-and-so. Now and then he would bewail the fact that he had not been able to gather more cases, and once he told me that the job was really too much for one man, especially for a fellow who was old and sick. "You see that wall?" he asked, pointing to the side of a large room in the University Library, a space at least thirty by fifty feet; "what I'd like to do would be to cover that wall-space, or a bigger one, with drawers and then set a lot of men to work filling them with notes. Up and down would be tribes and peoples. Crosswise would run topics, like property, marriage. There'd be a third dimension, too; the length of the drawers. Then we'd get somewhere, after a while!"

We students knew that Sumner was working incessantly in his collecting; and industry in the teacher breeds diligence in the student. We began to collect too; and here we had the benefit of urgent precept; for he solemnly warned us off "from all the costly errors I've made. I've had to abandon two systems of note-taking before I worked out this one." He used to adjure us to begin always by setting the reference at the head of any excerpt, "before you get excited and forget it, and then sometimes have to spend hours hunting it up and very likely never find it again—the way I've done so many times." He spoke like a veteran naturalist explaining to a novice how to track some elusive insect. I think the joy of the chase—after facts—was in him a kind of passion. Indeed, it allured him over-long, for he did not live to write very much of his treatise. It seems to me that he liked to collect better than to synthesize. When his hand became crippled so that writing was out of the question, he went back to his reading with a resignation and even contentment that could scarcely have been foreseen. That he could not go on with composition—the labor of which, in addition, he said, immeasurably exhausted him—seemed to prey on his mind far less than I, for one, had expected. "I shall never finish it," he said of the projected treatise on *The Science of Society,* with conviction, yet not sadly. "*Folkways* is my last book. The rest is your job. I'll give you all my notes and other stuff and you go ahead." There was, in his voice if not in his words, certainly a trace of relief.

It is true enough that most undergraduate students know little, and care less, about what their instructors are doing in their workshops; but for a mature or maturing man who has chosen his line of endeavor and acquired the professional interest, it is highly stimulating to see his mentor active in the field. I do not mean prolific in publication, much less an object of applause from outsiders; that counts, of course, in its degree, but it is not vital to

student estimate; I mean seriously and disinterestedly at work—
sincerely, single-mindedly intent upon the laborious search for
truth. Sumner was all of that. For some years after he had turned
from political economy, he had published little, "because," as he
told a pert reporter who asked the reason for his silence, "I'd
rather correct my own mistakes than have somebody else correct
them for me." It did not worry us that he did not publish, for we
could see the magnitude of his task. All that we feared was that he
could not complete it—a justified misgiving. And in particular we
used to snort at those who hinted that Sumner was through and
would never do anything more; that he had shown both poor judgment and probably oncoming senility when he deserted a man's-
size subject like economics to dabble about with Hottentots, and
"mores," and "societology."

Once, as a graduate student, I asked Sumner whether I had not
better take a visiting economist's course. "He's got a soft spot in
his head like the rest of 'em," was the reply, "but it won't hurt you
much." Of a course in the relation of economics and ethics: "Yes,
take it. There's no relation between the two, but you can listen to
what he says." He thought economics was "becoming metaphysical" and said he had registered a vow never to write a textbook on
the subject.

There were not a few who wasted varying amounts of benignant,
rueful, or tolerant pity upon Sumner, while he was working out his
latter phase. Nobody who knew what he was up to had any such
sentiment. Uninformed critics, dependent for their wisdom upon
hearsay or sheer intuition, pronounced that Sumner's results
would be out-of-date before they were published—inasmuch as he
was a Spencerian, and Spencer was out of date. It always inspired
us with scornful hilarity to think of Sumner as the worshipful
disciple of anybody. We were as little sorry for him as we were,
in retrospect, for Darwin during that score of years while the
Origin was in the making. And we suspected that those who jaun-
tily relegated Spencer to the junk-pile had picked up their knowledge of him second hand. We had heard an eminent historian,
George B. Adams, in the course of an attack on "sociology,"
qualify his strictures by saying that the view Spencer had given of
society as a whole and in the articulation of its parts had made it

impossible for history ever again to be written as it had been before Spencer's time. We saw that Sumner had embarked upon one of those solitary and lengthy enterprises which yield no immediate results; and we knew him to be the sort of a man who would not issue bulletins or otherwise self-advertise. He never felt that "the world" was all agog over his next publication. His work was his own business, to be talked about when done, not before. It was a good many years before *Folkways* slipped quietly into print. Of that book he said to me: "I'm spending a lot of time on it. I don't know whether it's a gold mine or just a big hole in the ground. I shall never know. That's for the rest of you to decide." *Folkways*, he said, was the only book he had written, not at the behest of a publisher. "I hope that they [Ginn and Company] will sell *Folkways* but I do not expect that the market will take many. . . . No one can dab in it and write anything about it and I think that anyone who reads it must give time to it. I have been reading parts of it and am as well satisfied with it as a man ever is."

There was nothing showy about Sumner's scholarship, nothing portentous or esoteric, nothing oracular. There was no parading or drum-majoring at all. He was a worker, like other workers, using tools available to anyone who had the diligence to learn how to manipulate them. The way to get at the truth was not by juggling the opinions of authorities or the bright ideas of pseudo-authorities and splitting the differences or discovering some golden, reconciling mean; it was not by devising "methods" and "technique"; it was by sitting down and studying the facts hard and long. Sumner used to say that if Spencer had had "those notes up in my attic," the *Principles of Sociology* would have been something much better; and he would bewail the fact that he lacked Spencer's easy style to help him set forth his own conclusions.

WHEN he was reading, Sumner's posture was somewhat like that of one seated on the back of his neck. He had a large stuffed chair, up to which he drew a special, unclassifiable piece of furniture designed, I imagine, by himself, with a kind of low lectern, into which he had screwed several contrivances to keep his book open before him. He slid this reading-device over his knees, or else slid his body under it, and, having within reach everything he was likely to need, pegged away in a position that gave one the backache to observe. When he wrote, he shifted to a desk and sat bolt upright upon an uncomfortable wooden stool. I do not think he ever planned anything for pure comfort, in connection with his labors, but aimed only at what he considered efficiency and time-saving.

While I think of it, I may say that I never saw him engaged in any manual labor whatsoever, such as gardening, repairing something about the house, or even blowing up his bicycle-tires. I think he regarded such jobs as somebody else's, quite out of his line. Once, when he found me wheeling a barrow, his remark was: "Well, I don't see but you do that as well as any dago could."

I suppose many of Sumner's admirers are familiar with the strong, characteristic script that he wrote. It might be interpolated that his typewriting, of which he did none in later years, was atrocious: he would strike the wrong keys, or miss them altogether, over and over again; and apparently he made no attempt to correct his errors, if the sense was recognizable. But his handwriting was neat and crisp to the last degree and, once one had familiarized himself with it, legible, despite his tendency to abbreviate. His writing, earlier in life, was much more rounded and less angular. It is perhaps unnecessary to say that his script, after he began to train his left hand and, later, to use his right again, was shaky and often hardly legible.

In his haste to keep up with his thought, he hit upon many obvious and a good many symbolic abbreviations. Regularly he used "&" and "&c"; also "w" (with), "wh" (which), "wd" (would), "shld" (should), "eno" (enough), "durg" (during), and so on. His version of "yours truly" appears in the letter reproduced elsewhere (p. 74). Though, apparently, he had never contemplated learning shorthand, he had a whole series of what I have called symbols, some self-explanatory, others not. The Hebrew letter *aleph*, conventionalized to "א" meant himself, "I," "W. G. Sumner"; *beth* stood for "property," *lamedh* for "trade." I think that his table of signs is odd and interesting enough to be reproduced in an approach to completeness.

Male	husband	Function	Anthropological
Female	wife	Structure	Society
Mankind		Integration	Societal
Anthropos		Education	Social
Educational value		Civilization	Pleto
Criticism or filosofy		Religion	Paleo
No Non-		Marriage	
Kin		State	
Population		Sex	
Superstition		Evolution	Family
God		Colonial	Father fam.
Nature		Effects of	Mother fam.
Philosofy		Agency	
Organization		Beast	
History		Water	
Vice Versa		Magic	
Lack of		Mode or method of	
Race		Custom	
Economic		Individual	
Fire		Peace ~~~~	Asia
Trade		Taboo	Africa
Plenty			America
Covenant		Anthropology	Europe
War		Somatic	Australasia
Struggle for Existence		Anthropografy	France
Compet. of life		Somatology	England
Barbarism		Ethnografy	U.S.
Liberty		Ethnology	Germany
Equality		Histor. Anthrop.	
Political & Civil		Societology	
Group		Demografy	
Property		Demology	
Notions about			
Pain			
Pleasure		Stat. Auth.	Societology
- ism		Self - maintainance	
- tion		Self - perpetuation	
- ness		Self - gratification	
- ology		Mental Reaction	
- ografy		a) Mental Outfit	
- ity		b) Societal System	
- ability			
- ment			
- ization			
- ing			
- ies)			
- ation		Industry	Race characteristic
- ship		Information	Culture
- ocracy		Intelligence	Healing; Cure
- hood		Communication	Soul
- ous		Transmission	Environment
- age		Vital	
Amulet		Death (af.)	
Ceremony		Mortuary	Physical
Death		Institution	Metaphys or supraorganic
Prehistoric		Luck	
		Sacrific	Definition
Beginning of		Worship	
Sacred		Relations	
Mores		Making	
		Various	Nation
		Sundry	National
		Assort. of	Societal Significance of
			Element

-ocracy
Society
Policy of
Manifestations
Demonstration

GHJK   RTV
NN'₂   XX'₂

In writing he ran his words together, not lifting his pen, often for several inches, and sprinkling in a number of these signs along the way, so that to the uninitiated his manuscripts looked rather esoteric in spots. A not too intelligent copyist of his unfinished manuscripts emerged, after much bewilderment, with some startling passages.

One of the reasons for the invention of such signs lay in the narrow space available upon the projections of the cards he used as topic-headings in his note-files. There were a lot of these headings, and he was very careful to see that they stood out to the eye, not lurking one behind the other. By use of his signs he could get a great deal upon a small projection of cardboard: for instance " ⚥ & ⌿ " (marriage and property), " y ℓ " (ideas about the soul). These more complicated symbols and combinations do not appear in the manuscripts.

He used cardboard of several colors and was much vexed if the tints faded, speaking with marveling appreciation of a secretary of his who restored the colors of the exposed label-projections by pasting thin paper, colored durably, over the bleaching cardboard projections. He used also note-slips, of a size peculiar to himself ($8\frac{1}{2} \times 4\frac{1}{2}$ inches), of various tints. Regular excerpts from books were taken on white; bibliography was red; his personal comments and observations were on green sheets; topic-outlines were on yellow; and so on. In his vexation at encountering notes, later on, from which, in his haste or preoccupation, he had left out the exact reference, he bought himself a number of fonts of rubber-faced type, and carefully set up titles of books and journals, printing them at the head of a sheaf of blank notes before he or his copyist began to make the excerpts he had marked lightly in pencil during his reading of a book or article.

He was much concerned about the safety of his collections. One time, he said, there had been a fire next door and he had toiled up and down the winding stairs, to and from his third-story study, carrying down his heavy drawers of notes. "I got 'em all out there in the back yard and it nearly killed me. Then I found that the fire was out. I hired someone to lug 'em back."

He told me that his secretarial expenses were about twenty dollars a month, for nine months in the year, and that he made his copyist—"my woman," he called her—take her work home to do, because the constant tapping of her machine irritated him.

"Why doesn't the good man dictate?" someone inquires, "especially now that his hand is lamed?" "Can't," replied Sumner, tersely, when I asked him that; "makes me windy." There is a lot in that diagnosis. A lawyer once reported that he had been going over briefs antedating the stenographer and typewriter, and that he was amazed at their brevity and condensation as compared with later, dictated papers. We are likely to become expansive when a worshipful hireling is gaping, pencil poised, for the next weighty word; and, becoming uneasy if we keep her waiting, we are likely to run into verbosity. Spencer, it is true, dictated all his books after the first, but it has seemed to many of us that he would have done better if he had not been obliged to dictate, for, despite his clarity, there is an irritating monotony about his style, akin, remotely perhaps, to the over-regular meter of Pope. And Spencer is, at least occasionally and despite his fecundity of thought, expansive and even wordy. To those who want to revise their sentences a good deal as they go, dictation is virtually out of the question. Sumner was not of that type, for his manuscripts show comparatively few emendations, verbal or in phraseology, though many interpolations of sentences and paragraphs; but he realized that there was danger in dictation, and he was not used to it when his greatest need for it came upon him. Further, I think he wanted always to be alone when he was writing. In any case he dismissed the suggestion about dictating with brusque decisiveness.

He spread before him his wide sheets of unruled, thick, expensive paper (about $14 \times 8\frac{1}{2}$ inches), with a vertical blue line about four inches from the right-hand margin—the space thus set off being reserved for emendations and footnotes, provided the latter were not mere references, in which case they went right in with the text—and wrote rapidly across the remaining ten inches, straight away, in his somewhat angular hand, the lines being likely always to incline upwards. The space to the right was often not large enough to contain his additions and the back of a sheet might be covered with writing, in a hand growing finer and finer as space threatened to give out. This part of his manuscripts is cruel to the eye, though he seems never to have sensed that for himself.

Having completed a section of manuscript, he ran brass clips through two holes punched near the left margin (he had provided himself with a powerful punch, in case he needed other holes), labeled the section with great letters or symbols upon a blank first page, and laid it aside. He did not number his pages, so that if they escaped their bonds by any chance it was often a miserable job to arrange them again.

I am led to say in this connection, that Sumner was always rather extravagant when it came to the materials he used in his work. He bought very expensive paper and notebooks. "That's no good," he pronounced, rather disdainfully, of some note-paper I had been economical about. "Too thin and cheap. 'T won't stand up—get's dog-eared, wrinkled, mussy. It don't pay to get poor stuff."

Sumner's handwriting, it seems to me, correctly reveals the strength and forthrightness that characterized the man.

It occurs to me that I never heard Sumner, as I have heard so many other teachers, complain of student handwriting—or, indeed, of anyone else's. "Your writing's clear enough," he would say, "better than mine." He deprecated the old-fashioned German typography, but apparently only on general principles. I must attribute this, again, to his seemingly tireless vision; and also, perhaps, to his method of reading, which was so rapid that it must have involved taking in stretches at a time, and fastening only upon essentials—for he did not miss anything, so far as I could see. Certain books he read very painstakingly and with copious annotation, notably Lippert's *Kulturgeschichte;* and he made exhaustive digests in small notebooks of such works as he used in classes, for instance, Ranke's *Der Mensch.*

IN graduate work with Sumner, we perceived little or nothing of the "dogmatism," if it be so called, of his lectures in his elementary course, and nothing of that "intellectual arrogance" of which he has been accused. He had no great opinion of his own accomplishments, but acted like a man who faced a task so large that whatever he might do could be but little. He cited his own limitations, from time to time, and was solicitous that we should avoid the pitfalls into which he had slipped. He welcomed new facts with eagerness and, it sometimes seemed, was over-credulous of certain novel interpretations, such as that of a Russian writer who thought the Yakuts saw the evils of human in-breeding from their experience with cattle. His attitude was, to my mind, humble—certainly far from arrogant. It is my opinion that this impression of intellectual arrogance was derived from Sumner's impatience of ignorant cocksureness; for he always bristled up when he encountered pretension, affectation, or sham, and doubtless replied curtly to many a *poseur*. I am not apologizing for his mode in retort, which was not suave; I have myself, more than once, been the object of his blunt disapprobation, freely expressed, though it was never such as to hurt my feelings at all; but I am stating, with no qualifications, that he was the opposite of overbearing when one was working beside him.

He had always a deep sympathy for self-supporting students, for, though he had not been one of them, he knew what poverty was. He used to advise newly arrived graduate students who consulted him about his courses that, in a climate like New Haven's, they ought to wear a light overcoat in the spring and fall.

He was considerate; helpful—for instance, in keeping a student's or colleague's needs in mind, calling attention by post card to new books relating to his main interest; encouraging; comforting in adversity. I shall never forget an early lecture of mine which was a dismal failure so far as interesting the audience was concerned. Many filed out under cover of the darkness, while some slides were being shown. The next morning I was melancholy and told Sumner that I had fallen down flat. "I was there," he replied, to my astonishment, for, during those days of ill health, he seldom went out in the evening. "I don't think it was a failure. I'd like to set a question on that lecture to those people who went out." And then he told me what was the matter with the delivery and how to correct it. "When you are showing slides, stand sideways to your audience, not with your back to it, and speak up as if you thought them important, even though you don't." Then: "But it wasn't a failure, and don't you think so!" he wound up, stoutly.

On one occasion he rated me soundly, and justly, for a poor year's work. In a graduate course of his, covering the early financial, political, and social history of the United States, he had assigned seven volumes of outside reading for doctorate candidates. One of these was his own *History of Banking in the United States,* a huge volume, full of unrelieved detail and, as I think, the most carelessly done of all his writings. (The secretary employed by him once told me that he often grew impatient while at that task, and would hand her a sheaf of notes, saying: "Here! Just run these in as they come." His attention was being diverted at the time from economics, and I think the task of writing this book was a sour one.) In any case, this was the seventh volume prescribed; and, since there were only two copies available for a number of us, no one could have the book very long.

I was one of the first to get a copy, and I tried to read it. But I could not—or did not; and finally it had to go to someone else. I did not try to get it again; for, aside from a complete lack of interest in it, I figured that it was only one of seven, and decided to let it go. But when the examination came, in June, every question upon the list of seven volumes was upon the *Banking.* Having done the best I could on the body of the examination, I omitted the doctorate questions, stating my opinion of the book and the theory upon which I had passed it up; I wrote that I was fully prepared upon Weeden's *New England,* Bruce's *Virginia,* and Sumner's own *Finance and Financier of the American Revolution,* which made up the other six volumes. I was irritated rather than frightened, and probably showed it. I thought the concentration upon the one book unfair, and said so.

Silence ensued until the fall; then he lit on me. He had a right to do so, aside from the examination matter; for, owing to various circumstances, none of which he knew, I had been irregular in work throughout the preceding year. He told me that I had disappointed him; in brief, he got after me in his sharp-stick fashion. He not only prodded me; he also pounded; and I had nothing to say, for I knew I had not done well. While I listened, I considered resigning my fellowship at once, and doubtless looked pretty chopfallen.

At length he stopped and eyed me sharply. "Now," he resumed, after a pause, "don't—take—this—too—seriously. You've been splashing around. A good many do it. Irving Fisher splashed around for quite a while, like a puppy in a millpond. I splashed around myself, a lot longer than he did." He paused again; then, feeling that he had perhaps diluted the dose too much, snapped: "Now, no more of this foolishness!" And he rose and saw me in silence to the door. "I'll try to," said I. "All right. Good night," he growled, and shut the door conclusively. His "all right" sounded to me a good deal like: "You'd better!"

For a year or more he eyed me suspiciously and was rather distant and implacable. I tried to talk my thesis subject over with him, but got nowhere. He listened to my plans noncommittally; I could not see that he was either pleased with or critical of them, or even interested. This was, I suppose, an exhibition of his "hands-off" attitude; later on, he used to say that I "coddled" my graduate students too much, by conferring with them and "letting them run all over" me. " 'T isn't good for them—or you."

I finished my thesis by myself and after my own devices and handed it in. In a couple of days, on a Monday morning, I received a post card, which I still have. It begins without ceremony. "I have spent all day Sunday over yr thesis. There can be no question of its merit & acceptance. Come & get it any P.M. at 2 or ev'g at 7. I want to talk it over a little. W. G. S."

I went at seven. He brought out the manuscript, which was loose leaved, in a typewriter-paper box, and shuffled it over briefly, saying little or nothing. Finally: "Who did this typewriting?" he asked. "I did." "Very good typewriting," he commented, and handed the box to me. I recall no further reference to the thesis until, several years later, when it was in press, he asked me to let him have the author's galleys, "to cut up for my notes."

The thesis was on Homeric society and contained many passages clipped from the Teubner text and pasted in. It turned out that he had compared all these passages with the English translation, to be sure that the conclusions tallied.

I used to get pretty resentful toward him now and then, during that early period; but I was given grace to realize that I deserved most of the gruff admonitions and reproofs that I got, and for the rest—well, it was Sumner's way, and that was all there was to it. You might as well resent the precession of the equinoxes. He was the biggest man I had ever encountered, and he was ill and miserable. He never ceased to emit bluntly what was in his mind, and when we disagreed, he generally said spicy things; but he never hurt my feelings or humiliated my self-respect. After a while, one saw that there was, in his rough expressions, a certain grim humor that, as I have said, his eyes did not betray. "You ought to *try* not to be a damn fool!" or "I won't talk to you any more; I'll talk to your wife; she's got ten times the sense you have." In a letter: "It is great fun to sulk and you do it well but it is d—d folly." Again: "I did not like your last letter to me. I held my reply in pickle until I should see you. I cannot keep things in pickle so my reply is only getting soft. Let me remonstrate with you about the sulky way of giving up to opponents. I have done too much of that. It never brings any good result, and it spoils your temper. Next winter we will go to work in time and try to get what you want. Do not look at it any other way." Such outbreaks, on occasions when he became exasperated because I could not be persuaded to see life "sensibly," were his way of showing interest. I much prefer them, in retrospect, to what he called "soft-soaping," for the sincerity behind them was as rugged as the expressions.

I RETURN to the loose chronological strand upon which I am stringing casual recollections. Once I sounded Sumner upon the prospects of my staying on at Yale. His answer was that I must count on nothing; that he could not say a word that would in the slightest limit his freedom of choice when the time came; that the next man needed was a professor of Demology, then of Somatic Anthropology; that I must hang on to the edge of things till I got a chance—in Greek or in anything else that would support me—and meanwhile get ahead with my studies as fast as I could. This was discouraging, but it represented the exact and scrupulously stated truth; I have often contrasted his strict honesty with the empty hopes that have been idly, to save trouble or in pure cowardice, held out to other men I have known. Sumner talked to me with the rough candor that Dr. Eliot exhibited to Dean Briggs; and I feel toward him in the matter as Dean Briggs says he feels toward his departed chief. Thank God for the vertebrates in the species *Homo!*

In a certain faculty meeting, I am told, Sumner stated some plain truth bluntly. There was a protest. "Well," retorted Sumner, "it's the truth." "Yes," replied someone, "but the truth should not be spoken at all times." "That's never been my idea," Sumner growled. As regards speaking of the truth of the dead, he used to say that truth should not stop at the grave, and falsehood begin.

When, at Sumner's instance, I had finally been offered a small position in the economics department, he said to me: "Now you've got a foothold; hang on!" He reflected awhile, then: "Just strictly between us, you don't know much economics." "No," I replied, "less than none." He eyed me a moment. "But you know more than the students. Don't forget that."

Later on, he suggested that I offer a course to Juniors, introductory to his Senior course. I said: "You have taught me all I know and I'm afraid I shall unconsciously encroach on your course." "Don't ever let that worry you," he said. I told him that, in an economics course of which I was quiz-master, the term "evolution" having turned up, I had asked how many felt they had a good grip on that theory; and that, of some seventy men, only a half dozen had raised their hands—and that some of those had pulled them down hastily when they saw how few there were. "That's the ticket!" Sumner exclaimed, "give them a good dose of Darwin. That's good for anybody." For several years thereafter, this introductory course, called "Anthropology," was regularly referred to by the students as "Evolution." So far as I know, it was the first large course to present, in Yale University, the Darwinian Theory. Later, as better presentations of evolution were developed, the whole treatment shifted toward societal evolution.

One Sunday a fellow student who had been taken into the Trinity Church choir, came in upon us and, panting briefly, burst out: "Who do you think I saw down to Trinity this morning, passing the hat?" We admitted ignorance. "It was Old Bill!" he declared. "Big as life, all dressed up in his Sunday jeans, and mighty impressive, if you ask me!" "Gosh!" we all chorused. Some of us had not known that Sumner was a clergyman, and those who knew that he had been, at one time, supposed the phase long past. We used to wonder what he really believed. So far as I ever heard, he had never attacked religion or treated it lightly; but he had certainly been wholly impersonal in his handling of the religious element along with the other social factors.

This is not yet the place to consider the whole matter of Sumner's religion, or absence of it; but I wish to record here our student impression. We were certainly surprised that Sunday afternoon to learn of his official connection with the church, and debated long and acrimoniously upon the issue suggested; namely, whether a man whose sentiments toward religion were what we assumed Sumner's to be could, with propriety, continue to be a clergyman. Later, someone looked up the exact connection Sumner had with the Episcopal Church and found that he was reported as detailed to Yale College as a teacher. It always seemed to me that he handled the evolution of religion, in his classes, with marked reserve; so that while he was constantly abused for his views on economic and political subjects—the tariff, sound money, expansion, and so on—and once grossly misrepresented by a New Haven paper as to his views on the family, no one called him an atheist or even an agnostic. I think this indicates that he had been much less outspoken when it came to religion; and I believe there were reasons both general and personal for his reticence, though I do not for a second infer that he held his tongue because of fear, either of abuse or anything else. I shall return to this topic in another connection.

Sumner was abused enough, and we all knew it. It failed to hurt him any, in our eyes. We heard that he had a whole deskful of letters, received over many years, in which he was compared, to his disadvantage, with "that other Sumner" (Charles), who was a patriot, and was called chosen names, such as "arrogant jackass." Dr. Starr reproduces certain of these offerings. We heard too that when Sumner felt a little down in the dumps, he used to get out his *Schimpflexicon* and chuckle over it. We loved him for all this.

In this connection, or lack of connection, I am reminded of his diary. He kept one for years, jotting down a line or two each day. He told me that it had proved very useful in an unexpected way. "No matter how miserable I feel, I can always turn back and find a time when I felt worse."

THERE can be little doubt that he liked a fight—probably in some part because of the artistic pleasure of using his own incomparable weapons. I recall a classic occasion when one of his displays of fearlessness roused us all to frantic admiration. It was during the excitement and swelling self-satisfaction consequent upon the naval engagement at Santiago, the reduction of Manila, and the acquisition of those "Pearls of the Tropic Seas," the Philippines. Sumner chose this juncture to emerge from a long retirement, succeeding his breakdown, with an address entitled, cryptically but belligerently: "The Conquest of the United States by Spain."

He appeared in rather old-fashioned evening clothes, with stiff, bulging shirt bosom, his tie sprawling and apparently about to come unloosed, his hair clipped tight to his head, and looking, as usual, as if he had just emerged from an orgy with much soap and hot water. He moved up to a kind of music rack upon which he deposited his manuscript with firmness. He reached for his glasses, sweeping the packed hall the while with a kind of complacently sardonic glance. I think he was not introduced at all, or merely with a word. The audience applauded, but he made no response, merely waiting for silence. Then he lit into the pet imperialistic views of the time, shared by nearly everybody present. For awhile there was no applause, but he kept on driving in the knife and then turning it. His air was as of one who should say, gripping a resisting nose and forcing open reluctant jaws: "I've got you here, and down it goes!"

This address may be read by one who desires, among Sumner's *Collected Essays;* although the striking personal element is not there, I think the essence of its pugnacious challenge has not evaporated away. It was not long, that evening, before a kind of thunderstruck silence was broken by applause which increased in volume and strength all through the remainder of the reading. (I might say that Sumner's effectiveness never lost much from the presence of a manuscript; he eyed his audience sternly most of the time, taking but fleeting glances at what he had before him; and the perching of his glasses upon his nose and their off-snatching was an integral part of the effect.) No one present will ever forget the solemn tone or the dramatic gesture of his long arm and hand, as he pronounced the words: "And yet this scheme of a republic which our fathers formed was a glorious dream which demands more than a word of respect and affection before—it—passes—away." At the end, when he bowed, jerking his head forward about two inches, and his long fingers seized upon his manuscript, the clapping and shouting were deafening. Then he retired, with the sketch of a grim smile, and another slight inclination. The comments of those emerging from the hall were tributes as to a Roman soul.

A young man who was cultivating *The Yale Law Journal* took his nerve in his hands the next day and begged the address from Sumner. He got it, though Sumner ruefully remarked that he had meant to sell it and thought he might have got a hundred dollars for it.

In his preface to *Protectionism*, Sumner speaks of men "who may not be answered when they come into debate, because they are 'great' men, or because they are 'old' men, or because they have stock in certain newspapers, or are trustees of certain colleges. All these [he enumerates several other classes of adversaries] have honored me personally, in this controversy, with more or less of their particular attention. I confess that it has cost me something to leave their cases out of account, but to deal with them would have been a work of entertainment, not of utility." Elsewhere Sumner remarks that anyone who starts to whine and cry when the blows begin to fall had better have kept out of the fight altogether.

He appealed to at least one socialist, a drug-clerk who spent his savings on books. "Do you know the essays of Sumner?" this gentleman asked me. "Yes, I've read them," I replied. "I like Sumner," he said. "But," I objected, "he attacks all your pet beliefs." "Yes, but he *can hit so hard!*"

I do not say that Sumner sought conflict, or was spoiling for it; but I think he entered it with considerable zest, provided he believed thoroughly in the righteousness of what he was going to fight for. There is a story bearing upon this last consideration. On a certain occasion, the Freshman debating team, having the choice of opposing or defending a given contention, had been advised to take one side of the question because it was tactically preferable.

By some chance, the question was referred also to Sumner, who promptly advised them to take the other side. The issue of strategy was cited. "No matter!" said Sumner. "One thing's false and the other's true. You want to stand for the truth." He was then told that their official adviser would not coach them if they chose sides contrary to his advice. "All right," answered Sumner. "Let him go. I'll coach you myself." And so he devoted a good many hours to these boys, probably scaring them half to death. It would be pleasant to record that all three judges of the debate concurred for Sumner's protégés, but alas! it was just the other way. Still, this anticlimax need not obscure the real moral of the tale.

I have spoken of Sumner's equipment for intellectual or forensic combat. It was immense. A distinguished American economist once wrote of Sumner that "the results of his experiences in the discussion of the relative merits and advantages of the systems of free trade and protection have been such that probably no defender of the latter would now be willing to meet him in a public discussion of these topics." There were few enough who cared to meet him in discussion on any stage. He was a devastating debater, an incomparable duelist. His weapon seemed to be the double-handed sword and the rapier at the same time, the one being capable of metamorphosis into the other in the twinkling of an eye. He generally began with the latter and wound up with the former. In faculty discussions, according to one of his contemporaries, Sumner generally started off by being provocative (pinking his adversaries in tender spots, distributing minor smarts); then as the rest grew hot, he became cooler, and, in the end, dominated the situation. On occasion he developed an appalling frankness and moved into the tabooed range of personalities, but not without warning. It was as if, when he switched to the broadsword, or war-club, he roared: "Look out now! I'm coming after you!" before he charged. But he was not strong on amenity. He was rough—often very rough. His eye was always on the objective, and he did not swerve if some adult male person was in his way. And if he seemed to be cornered, he still could raise a laugh, by some dextrous turn; and when the situation had cleared he was firmly intrenched again.

One winter day a case of discipline was on the docket. Sumner had come in late and sat with his overcoat collar up, apparently not yet warm. Presently he expressed a positive opinion upon the case. A discussion which appeared to leave him bored and listless went on for some time; then other aspects emerged that seemed to stir him, and he expressed with equal positiveness an opposite opinion. "How does Professor Sumner reconcile his present statement with what he said when he first came in?" queried a colleague who disagreed with that second thought. Sumner turned to face the questioner and replied without a smile: "I don't reconcile them. I withdraw the first." I have seen many another man, in a similar situation, fumble about for rags of explanation to cover his nakedness of inconsistency.

On one public occasion he debated with a minor statesman who had considerable manner, together with luxuriant side-burns. This man came upon the platform urbanely, smiling, bowing, and rubbing his hands together in the approved style of the suave diplomat. His speech was of the type belonging with his preliminary warm-up. When Sumner's turn came, he too advanced mincingly, grinning sardonically, and winding his incredibly long fingers about. The unfitness of his face and form to such evolutions smote the audience where it lived; and his reply was as withering as his entrance had been deliberately grotesque.

Sumner was quite willing to receive blows or to take things back. The grand case of retraction, or explanation of himself, occurred at a dinner given by their colleagues to Sumner and two others, Dean Wright and Professor Perrin, all of whom retired in 1909. Sumner spoke last. I recall two passages in particular from his speech. He praised the Yale professors' method of recruiting our numbers, and said that it made for mutual confidence and good will. "*We—elect—each—other;* that's the reason," he pronounced slowly and impressively. He warned against executive encroachment upon this privilege: "We professors own the College." Then he moved on to consider our mutual relations. At length he paused and looked around the table, quizzically. "I see here," he went on, "a good many men that I have fought with, off and on. I am aware that I have often broken out like a boorish boy. But I never meant anything." The whole table laughed and applauded.

I might add that, seeing him the next day, I told him that he had made a fine speech. He muttered something deprecating, as usual; then made an admission. "When I got home last night, Mrs. Sumner was awake and asked me how I'd got on. I sat for a moment on the side of her bed, and I told her: 'Jeannie, I made the speech of my life.'"

When I asked Sumner how he had acquired his debating powers, he replied: "Oh, we fellows in college used to sit up half the night jawing over things." But this did not explain; for what thoughtful young college man has not spent many midnight hours in arguing, mainly in circles and without much of any information to constitute his right to an opinion, about all conceivable subjects? Of course, when I knew him, Sumner had a wealth of knowledge and experience to draw upon, and was thus triply armed; but there was more to it than that. Perhaps his outstanding power, in exposition as in controversy, lay in an uncanny insight, a deadly capacity for penetrating as if by some instinct, into the heart of an issue. This was inimitable and savored of the inexplicability of sheer genius. I do not know where he got it, but he seems to have been in possession of a large measure of it even in youth. It was correlative, I suppose, with his intense interest in questions at issue, his seriousness (which was, back in his boyhood, close to priggishness), and his power of concentration. He usually sought at once for the human element in any matter; the homely, everyday element of human nature. "I guess the Japs are fighting for their beans" was his terse comment on the Russo-Japanese conflict. Of an Oriental father who objected to his son's not marrying: "Got his eye on kingdom come." Of a mature man who exhibited a levity unbecoming to his years: "Guess he likes to hug the girls too much." Of protectionists: "They want to get their hands into other people's pockets."

Sumner's writings are spiced with observations of this order, so that sentimentalists have branded him as cynical. Of all things he hated "gush," and a sentimental wailer was to him, as he denominated Ruskin, "a whining old grandmother." Anyone who strips off the pretexts and rationalizations with which human beings are prone to disguise stark human nature, to point out the real motives of men, is always impatiently dubbed a cynic, or an enemy to progress, or a misanthrope. Sumner was no one of these;

but he did not believe in fooling himself or others, and he knew the human heart in its weaknesses and smallnesses. He knew its more generous qualities too; but, hating sham as he did, and having the spirit of the crusader, he spent his energy in revealing and assaulting the unworthy rather than in comfortable, and profitable, laudation of things as they are. If those who are now objecting to the statement of the truth about our national saints had heard of his strictures of years ago, they would have united with certain political partisans, upon whose exposed toes Sumner had set a heavy heel, in declaring that his death or dismissal was Yale's most crying need.

I recall standing with Sumner, late one afternoon, on a hilltop overlooking New London harbor. We had paused to admire the deep blue of the sea against the land. Suddenly, out from the harbor there swept into that blueness, gleaming white in the light of the low sun, the battleship "Olympia." Several miles away, she moved with stately swiftness across our line of vision. "Let's wait a moment," I suggested. "That is a fine sight." "Yes," chuckled Sumner. "Better take a good look at her. There's some of your money in her."

WHEN a young fellow's instructor can reduce complicated issues to their simple elements, as Sumner could and did, and thus render understandable and cleancut the groundplan of a bewildering superstructure, there is no end to the confidence and loyalty with which he will be followed when it comes to the detailed analysis of the superposed tangle of flying buttresses, towers, and architraves. Sumner was strong on sketch-maps and perspectives. We knew where we were, and were going, all the time. In the midst of the tracking through detail—consider the shilling of Massachusetts Bay—he would recurrently get out his sextant and chart and shoot the sun for us. His lectures, his debates, and his written expositions all bear the same stamp; they all go undeviatingly to the homely, understandable reality of things. And it need hardly be said that, in contrast with the prevailing superficiality and whimsicalness of most "reasoners," Sumner stood, and ever stands, apart.

It is true that, as students, we saw but little of Sumner's human qualities. We saw him in panoply, not in the softer garb of family or social life—as a redoubtable leader in the strife against ignorance, obscurantism, humbug, and jobbery rather than as a human being who ate and drank, paid bills, economized, rejoiced, sorrowed, and sympathized. The story has been often told—Sumner himself recounted it with much gusto—of the student who, having accepted with trepidation an invitation to dine at Sumner's home, returned to report excitedly: "He's nice to his family! He's kind to his wife and fond of his children!" I recall an occasion when Sumner told his graduate class how he had once, on one of his walks about Mt. Desert Island, come upon the body of a drowned man, and realized that he did not know how to resuscitate him. "Probably he had been dead too long," he said, "but I would have given everything I possessed to have known what to try to do." This struck us all as a new aspect of the man of steel. And when he remarked of the photograph of a native African girl that she had a pretty figure, it seemed to us that the remark was somehow out of character. In short, we knew little of Sumner as a human being; he was to us a kind of vast, impersonal figure, formidable in every way, an epitome of strength and courage, stoical, self-sufficing. Of course, we were all wrong, for we saw only in part and, at that, with eyes unaccustomed to dimensions such as his.

Yet another impression remains to be recorded out of student days with Sumner, namely, that of his personal fineness. The nurse who attended him during the long stretches of delirium that preceded his death has said that no word crossed his lips that a sensitive woman might not have heard. His physician has remarked that Sumner had, as respects pure-mindedness, the fineness of a woman. I think we sensed in him this special type of his general fastidiousness. As there was in him no pettiness, so there was no lowness—no streak of the ignoble.

Surveying as he did, with professional objectivity, sex and sex-mores, he wanted no women in his classes, and had few, if any, in my day. I recall an occasion when one appeared for a time. Sumner was scrupulously courteous to her, as he always was to women, but was evidently troubled. He would begin to read, generally to translate, one of his notes; then he would look uneasy, stop, scan what was coming, and say: "Well, I guess there's no more in this one," and pass on to the next. This went on for several weeks: then, one morning, he came in, looking rather relieved. "The young lady has left us," he announced. "Now I guess I'd better go back to some of those notes I left out." We grinned but he did not smile. What he had left out would presumably offend no emancipated maiden of today; it would not have embarrassed, it is likely, the scientific lady of that time; but to Sumner it was improper for a mixed class. And we thought no less of him for his scruples. Call them prudery, if you like, or a kind of handicap imposed by the prudery of that period—nevertheless, in this day, with its minimum of reticence, or even decency (doubtless a normal reaction against the prudery of aforetime) there are those of us who still think no less of him for his fastidiousness.

Of an illustration of the rapidity of numbers-increase, involving the case of a man whose wife had borne him first a single child, then twins, then triplets, but who, despite his consternation, could yet thank heaven it was an arithmetical, not a geometrical, progression that he was confronting, Sumner said: "I wouldn't have used that illustration, myself—there are other ways of presenting that idea."

To him there was nothing amusing about sex and reproduction. I think it seemed to him ignoble to view them from that angle. He detailed with complete seriousness the often ridiculous sex ideas and practices of savages, though I suspect that he edited his cases now and then, for among his notes are several where the ludicrous aspects have been graphically portrayed by the ethnographer. I can witness, however, to his amusement over the prudery of an elderly lady who was shocked by *Folkways*. "She said," he chuckled, "that she never thought Mr. Sumner would write an indecent book."

And as I came to know him more intimately, later on, I found that there had been no pose or suppression at all in his reticence. He told me how he had cut up and burned, in his study stove, a profusely and realistically illustrated German book, for "I was afraid the maids might get hold of it." He even pasted heavy paper wrappings around books like the *Libido Sexualis*, so that they could not be consulted in the departmental library by the casual student, at least without warning. He objected to the use of novels like *Esther Waters* as prescribed course readings. I sometimes wonder what he would have said about the fiction of the present day, with its "clinical realism." His comment would not have failed in pungency. I am not going to argue the matter of what a "sane and sound" attitude toward sex may be, or whether Sumner was over-nice in his reticence; at any rate, he, for one, kept his mind on what he took to be higher things. License, prostitution, and all the rest of those unpleasant matters, had to be known about, just as men must acquire knowledge about the plague; and, as I said, Sumner was thorough and objective in his study, here as elsewhere; but I think the subject-matter revolted him, and that he much preferred to work along other lines.

SUMNER once told me that a student of his, during his economics period, had amused him greatly by his efforts to curry favor through the frequent assertion, in his test papers, that all this country needed for its well-being was "free trade and hard money." That was, indeed, the war-cry of Sumner's earlier days. And he was assuredly a convinced champion of Capital. A graduate of the College once recalled a brief valedictory of Sumner's to his class: "*Get Capital!*" and wished he had taken it more to heart. Someone once told Sumner that his *Social Classes* was a "Hymn to Capital." "Perhaps it is," was his reply. "Why not?"

Chief among Sumner's favorite topics, during his later phase, were "private property and the monogamic family." It has struck me, at times, that his hatred of socialism (communism) was based largely upon his conviction that it meant the dissolution of the family. Again and again, he used to pull off his glasses and wag a long forefinger at us while he enforced the contention that property and marriage had always been, were, and always would be indissolubly correlated; and that if you struck at the private-property monopoly, you were sure to hit the other monopoly of monogamy. I do not know that communism roused his moral indignation as he said protectionism did, but it certainly caused him to fear for the family.

When I was collecting Sumner's unpublished manuscripts, of which there were a good many that had been laid aside and were yellowed with age, I came across an envelope labeled "Coöperative

Commonwealth." In it were a number of slips containing items supposed to have been culled from a socialistic newspaper of July 4, 1950. I printed a number of them in *The Forgotten Man and Other Essays,* against the advice of certain friends who said they were a mere burlesque. In view of what has since happened in Russia, they are something other than that; in any case, they are worth turning to for anyone who wishes to fill out his acquaintance with Sumner.

I may, perhaps, conclude the reminiscences I am roughly assembling around Sumner as a graduate teacher by mentioning *laissez-faire.* I think Sumner, like Spencer, was stressed to advocate a let-alone policy by a realization of the damage done through ignorant, often well-intentioned meddling. He knew, as many of his critics did not, that purposes cannot be transmuted or projected into expedient consequences except by knowledge; and, aware of the deficiency of knowledge in even the wisest, as only the sincere and ardent searcher after truth can be, he resented the light self-confidence of the voluble empty-head in setting out to make the world over. That the uninformed should set up as experts and leaders seemed to Sumner absurd; and the fact that they had been so regularly followed was, he was convinced, the cause of a goodly portion of humanity's woes. I never heard him sneer at any program contemplating better social adjustment, when it was on a scale modest enough to be controlled and tested or if it had been proposed in a scientific spirit by someone whose experience, knowledge, and sincerity could be trusted. He was not for keeping the capable engineer away from the machinery; it was the half-baked enthusiast and his dupes who were not to touch it.

Behind such a reasonable preference for expert interference—or none—there doubtless lay in his mind, as in that of every evolutionist, a deep-seated confidence in the inevitable attainment, eventually if not speedily, of adjustment through the action of vast, unerring, impersonal forces. But such a prospect is too remote to satisfy the desires or to meet the pressing needs of eager or suffering men. Something must be done; and while, as Sumner used to quote from Webster, "a strong conviction that something must be done is the parent of many bad measures," it can be, if backed by knowledge, common sense, and disinterestedness, the spur to more expedient policy. And Sumner was not behind when it came to reformation.

I have never understood how anybody short of a moron, if he knew even the most obvious facts about Sumner's activities, could accuse him, as he has been accused, of an attitude of fatalistic passivity, indifference to social weal, or callousness to human suffering. Unless it be assumed that an unremitting advocacy of civil liberty is to be construed as service to *laissez-faire*, I do not find Sumner, or Spencer either, deserving of all the epithets aimed at them by self-constituted champions of "progress." Each of these men was fighting all his life, and, what is more, studying and working, for the betterment of social conditions through the correct understanding of what they had been and were. I challenge anyone to name a prominent so-called advocate of *laissez-faire* who was not active against the abuses of his time. The instructed reformer ought to enshrine the memory of these traduced men of sense; an assault upon them merely indicates the kind of mind the attacker possesses. Spencer was something of an old maid and perhaps a little feline now and then; he may pall on one a little. But Sumner, with all his hard hitting—indeed, in good part, just because of it —ought to appeal to anyone who, in these times, prays: "O God, give us a Man!" And each of them fought on after the battle had been, to all appearance, lost. In 1908, Sumner was a delegate to a Free Trade Conference in London. His report was: "Free trade is right where we found it. All the speeches (including mine) were on generalities—peace, love, and prosperity. . . . I am glad it is over. One night's rest such as I got last night is worth it all."

In one sense, there is no sane policy in the world except *laissez-faire*, meaning submission to the inevitable. No man, by taking thought or churning many words, can make objects fall upward. They fall downward, and that is the end of it. That is something that has to be accepted. The natural sciences have attained their present honorable and trusted position by recognizing the existence of laws that cannot be abrogated, not by dreaming of conditions where laws do not exist or by yearning out utopias to which they propose to adjust a revamped "human nature." What science has done is to find out what the immutable conditions are and then cleverly adjust to them. Immutable conditions are too

strong for us; they have to be let go (*laisser-aller*). Lincoln, when
his secretary was charging up and down his office, puffing out
heated words over yielding to England in the affair of the Con-
federate commissioners, is said to have remarked mildly: "Dana,
if you had hold of the left hind leg of a female elephant, and she
wanted to go, would you let her go?"

A scientist who exhorted his audience not to stand any longer
for capillary attraction or osmosis would be haled to a sanatorium
for treatment, unless he were thought to be fooling. No one would
rise to propose a resolution condemnatory of a "natural law." I
trust that sometime, when many men who have patterned themselves after Sumner and Spencer, having worn themselves out in
colossal labors, shall have arrived at the detection of societal
laws—that then similar sentiments will prevail within the social
range; for it is thus only that mankind can attain to such knowledge of the immutable conditions of societal life that they can
evade suffering and win comfort by adjustment to them.

Sumner and Spencer, in despair and irritation over what their
insight had revealed to them, may have laid on too much color,
now and then. They may have exaggerated somewhat. They may
have been too savage to be politic, polite, persuasive, or ingratiating; but these are the faults of the pioneers in forlorn hopes.
Sumner wrote, in his *What Social Classes Owe to Each Other:* "A
drunkard in the gutter is just where he ought to be, according to
the fitness and tendency of things. Nature has set up on him the
process of decline and dissolution by which she removes things
which have survived their usefulness." Elsewhere he says of "the
old doctrine—*laissez-faire*": "Let us translate it into blunt English, and it will read, 'Mind your own business.' It is nothing but
the doctrine of liberty."

At this point and with the moan of one sick at heart, the sentimental uplifter drops a grand little classic, neglecting to read its
last chapter on "Wherefore We Should Love One Another." His
tender spirit is scarified; but his honesty is not improved by his
wrath or his welling tears. From now on, Sumner is by him pro-
claimed a gross materialist, cold of heart and indifferent to "altruism" and "service." "Great is the truth and it will prevail,"

1902

pronounced someone to Huxley: "Great is misrepresentation, and it will prevail," retorted the tart-tongued evolutionist. For behold! the gushing friend of mankind, who has shuddered at a phrase, tears it out of even its immediate context and, for the rest of his life, parades it in a whisper to his students or to the public as evidence of the kind of person the author is.

I am coming to what kind of a person Sumner was. There have been sturdy souls to whom his "doctrine of liberty"—which he identifies with *laissez-faire*—has been a lifelong light upon the path. When I asked one of Sumner's eminent students, President Kinley, of the University of Illinois, what he would advise me to reprint in one of the volumes of *Collected Essays*, he replied to this effect: "Everything Sumner ever wrote on Liberty."

I HAVE mentioned Sumner's attitude toward speculative philosophy. He thought the study of it had done him irreparable damage. I can recall hearing in his undergraduate lectures something as follows: "It is said of the So-and-so Tribe that they have no philosophy. Happy people!" But he never criticized a colleague to us, and the transparent references in philosophy courses to "purveyors of gross materialism," and so on, merely served to drive us into Sumner's arms, especially as he ignored all these assaults.

In the faculty, however, he did not withhold his hand. Once upon a time it happened that all the professorships of philosophy became vacant at about the same moment. An older colleague has related to me that Sumner appeared at the next professors' meeting in a kind of eager excitement. Early in the meeting he took the floor and began: "Now's—our—chance!" and proposed dropping the subject once and for all from the curriculum. Dr. Starr treats of this incident more fully than I can here.

In my day, philosophy was required of everyone in both Junior and Senior years; it was the only requirement to extend into those upper reaches. Sumner objected to the preferential treatment of any subject whatever—"putting up high tariff walls around it." When that manifest indulgence was dropped, he became less militant, though his convictions remained unchanged. "If the students take it now, at any rate we are not responsible. We don't cram it down their throats."

One summer afternoon, at Fisher's Island, Sumner was a little scant of breath as we climbed the hill. He hated to admit any such disability and, when he wanted to rest, used to pause and relate a story. Not far off was a clay cliff into which myriads of swallows had bored to make nests. Sumner asked whether I had ever heard the definition of philosophy given by the man on the Mississippi steamer. One passenger asked another if he could define philosophy. The latter tried, but his effort was rejected by the questioner, who asked, as they were passing some clay cliffs like those before us: "See those cliffs?" "Yes." "See the swallows' holes?" "Yes; what of it?" "Well, if you took away the cliff and left the holes, that would be philosophy."

On one of his note-sheets—I should say one dating from his middle life—Sumner wrote, evidently communing with himself: "I should not be bold eno to say that *all* metaphysics, filosofy, etc. are fantasies [to this point the ink has evidently dried of itself, being very black, the writer having obviously stopped to reflect— then, boldly, and with the ink-marks light, evidently blotted immediately], but they all should be viewed with suspicion."

III

DURING the earlier part of his life, Sumner took no regular exercise, he told me, except to walk to and fro between Edwards Street and the college. He worked long hours and there were no holidays. "I worked every day—Sunday, Fourth of July, Washington's Birthday, all of them." A tale is told of his going to Albany to give an address and repairing, during the late afternoon, to a study of documents in the state library, which he prolonged, omitting his dinner, till he had barely enough time to reach the hall where he was to lecture. During these years of strenuosity, he had a heavy college schedule—not like those of colleagues who repeated the same matter to several divisions and year after year, but all newly prepared and kept abreast of the time; he bore also a large share in college administration and was on many faculty committees; and he constantly gave addresses and wrote articles, in addition to the publication of a number of books. He was in local politics briefly—he used to refer to two waste periods of his life: "when I was a parson," and "when I was in politics"; and, during the last twenty years of his life, was very active and influential as a member of the Connecticut State Board of Education.

In connection with politics, I recall a pompous remark by the late Hon. N. D. Sperry, long congressman from Connecticut: "Studying with Sumner, are you? Well, he's an able man—an able man. We used to be in the same party, but he went the English way and I went the American way." Sumner's brief comment on Sperry was: "God forgive me! I once voted for him." Of another prominent man: "He was a grinning, good-natured imbecile [imbeceel]."

No human frame, even one as sturdy as his (an oarsman of about Sumner's age has reported his astonishment at finding that Sumner, in middle age, pulled a stronger oar than he could), could endure indefinitely such drafts on vitality as he drew. Before I came to know him, he had already paid a part of the penalty; he had broken down and been away for two years and had become the "half man" that he used ruefully to call himself. While I knew him, he scarcely ever went out in the evening and generally comported himself as a semi-invalid.

In his early sixties, he regained, it seemed to me, a portion of his former health; but presently he began to feel the approach of old age—the premature oncoming, for if he had taken better care of himself he should have been able to work on till he was in his eighties. After his breakdown, he did pay some attention to his physical self. Regular exercise having been prescribed, he took to a bicycle, and every afternoon, at about the same time, he issued from his house, clad in short trousers, and rode away. He pedaled long distances, pretty slowly but with his usual indomitable resolution; we used to meet him many miles from town, pumping steadily along with his cap drawn down over his eyes. One of his younger colleagues, desiring to talk with him and reluctant to ask for an interview during his jealously guarded working hours, sug-

gested joining him on one of these bicycle excursions. "I supposed," he reported, "that the old man toddled along a little way
and sat down somewhere, but I never saw anything of him except
his back and he led me clear out beyond Fair Haven. When we got
back to his house I was so tired that I said goodbye without
getting off. I was afraid I couldn't get on again."

The roads, in those days, were rough; you had to plow through
mud or sand and jolt in or over the ruts. Sumner did not seem to
be having a good time—rather to be plugging doggedly along because it was his duty; but he looked hardy and determined—re-
solved, if he had to do this odious thing instead of what he most
wanted to do, upon giving good measure. Still, I think he enjoyed,
after all, the getting out into nature; and, as he intimated, he had
a good chance to think as he pushed monotonously along. He liked
to be alone pretty well. Once, when he was about to start abroad,
"to walk through Wales," I asked him whether he wouldn't miss
companionship, whether he wouldn't like it better if he had someone along. "Yes," he replied. "Sometimes I'm lonely. I'd like company if I could dispense with it when I didn't want it."

It is reported that Sumner came in once, with his bicycle, to find
on the porch of his White Mountain hotel, a rather well-known
literary man of the effusive type. This paragon of sentimentality,
name of Mabie, greeted him gushingly. Something on this order of
interchange followed:

Paragon: "I see you've been riding your wheel, Professor."
Sumner: "Huh!"
P.: "The roads are pretty good, aren't they, Professor?"
S.: "On the contrary, they are damnable!"
P.: "But not so bad, Professor, that you can't ride on them?"
S.: "You said you saw me!"

This anecdote recalls another equally rude retort, pardonable,
however, by those who knew both participants. Once in faculty
meeting, someone used the word "epistemology." Sumner broke in,
spacing out his words in his indescribable fashion: "Epistemology!
What—is—*epistemology?*" A rather sulphurous gentleman, who
was not himself a philosopher but doted on Plato, being abraded
by Sumner's jeering tone, caught fire and flared in his characteristic manner. He remarked smartly: "I do not see, Mr. Chairman,

that there is any occasion to employ sarcasm over this termi-
nology. All disciplines have their special and distinctive termi-
nology. Indeed, perhaps Professor Sumner will admit that even
political economy has its special terms. I see no reason . . ."—
and so on, didactically, for some time. When he had finished,
Sumner regarded the speaker for a moment with an air of mock
humility, then remarked: "Now—I feel as if I were back in Sunday
school."

"What are we teachers of Greek going to do if Greek is no
longer required?" queried a colleague. "Do?" retorted Sumner.
"Learn something else and teach it. I've had to do that, twice in
my life." "Brute! The brute!" one of the discomfited was heard to
mutter, under his breath.

Some of Sumner's remarks to me about his colleagues, present
and past, were tart. One man in his department, he said, had
"crowded" him by using the same textbooks and "hogging" the
best hours; that he himself had not put up a fight over such petty
annoyances from a person of no manners but simply got out. Of
another, notorious for his indecision: "You see, every idea comes
to him in a fog, *and—whirling;* so he takes hold of it now from one
side and the next time from another, generally the opposite." Yale
presidents had "regularly construed their function to be that of
brakeman"; of Mr. Hadley (recently elected), "it cannot be said
that he is an obstructionist." Sumner had not been for Hadley—in
fact, had written him as soon as he had heard of his candidacy, to
say so—but "he is the only President we have and is doing much
better now than I thought he would. If he goes on like this, I'll
have to take back a good deal of what I have said."

Sumner once gave me two versions of an interview with an op-
ponent—from two different angles, it seemed. Coming through my
office, which was next to his, he remarked: "Well, I saw So-and-so
yesterday." "What did you say to him?" "I didn't say anything;
I just sat and looked at him." A few days later, he came through
again. "Did I tell you I saw So-and-so the other day?" "Did you?"
"Yes; and I *talked turkey* to him!" The two versions, I found out
later, represented consecutive phases of the same interview.

I am here reminded of a report Sumner once wrote as chairman
of a faculty committee. He felt pretty strongly in the matter, for

he thought the College was about to be put upon. I met him just before the meeting at which, he said, he was to report. The next day I asked him how it came out and he replied that there had not been time for his report, "and I'm mighty glad of it. I can make it a lot stronger by working it over again." The next Thursday I encountered him after the meeting and repeated my query. "Well, first they ruined my report," he complained; "they softened all the starch out of it, and then they kicked me out and appointed a mushy compromiser in my place. All my work has gone for nothing. But I'm glad I'm out of it now. I detest this pussy-footing around." One of his colleagues told me that they had spent about two hours disengaging the barbs that Sumner had imbedded in his report while improving it during the interval, and, fearing that he would break loose again, had discharged his committee and appointed a new one.

Sumner was not a tactician, and he despised compromise. His career in politics was brief. He speedily found, he says, that he was being played with because he did not know the rules of the game; and, as he did not care to learn them, he remained outside. He was not one of those "arrangers of things" in the college organization who are to be distinguished from the doers of things. He was never interested in "putting things over" or in securing a place "in the bandwagon." He did not mind being alone in the support of any issue, local or general. Hammond Lamont once wrote: "Professor Sumner's valiant fight for free trade—almost single-handed it seemed at one time—has won him my especial respect." He thought protectionism, currency-inflation, and imperialism wrong and hateful, and assailed them at sight, in all times and places, irrespective of the sentiment of the age. One should think of these facts when he is tempted to listen to detractors of Sumner as an exponent of *laissez-faire*.

I AM tempted to enlarge upon the emergence from obscurity of Sumner's "Forgotten Man," during the campaign of 1932. First, Mr. Roosevelt evoked him, though he did not get him right. Then Mr. Mills, correcting Mr. Roosevelt, "placed" the Forgotten Man, but neglected to say that, according to the creator of this character, one of the major pieces of jobbery that he, and the "Forgotten Woman," suffered under was the protective tariff. Letters from many places in the country have attested the jealousy felt for Sumner's memory by those who knew him to have been the lifelong champion of that forgotten pillar of the state who "works and votes—generally he prays—but his chief business in life is to pay. His name never gets into the newspapers except when he marries or dies. He is an obscure man. . . . As soon as he is drawn from his obscurity we see that he is just what each one of us ought to be. . . . It belongs to his character to save something. Hence he is a capitalist, though never a great one. He is a 'poor' man in the popular sense of that word, but not in a correct sense. In fact, one of the most constant and trustworthy signs that the Forgotten Man is in danger of a new assault is that 'the poor man' is brought into the discussion."

In 1883, Sumner wrote: "The type and formula of most schemes of philanthropy or humanitarianism is this: A and B put their heads together to decide what C shall be made to do for D. The radical vice of all these schemes is that C is not allowed a voice in the matter, and his position, character, and interests, as well as the ultimate effects on society through C's interests, are entirely overlooked. I call C the Forgotten Man."

Because of his insight, Sumner's essays remain timely; the simple, homely truth does not become antedated. Consider the Proverbs of Solomon. Man after man has recorded that he has been rereading these essays, to be astonished at their timeliness. Mr. Dwight W. Morrow stated, about ten years ago, that he had recently been asked what was the latest best thing on ship subsidies and had replied unhesitatingly: "Sumner's little article, 'Shall Americans Own Ships?' written in 1881." Witness also the article on "The Bequests of the Nineteenth Century to the Twentieth," written in 1901, and discovered and published twenty-three years after his death. The Democrats would have been well advised to have stood, in 1928 as in 1932, upon Sumner's tariff views, as voiced in the terse little *Protectionism*. One prominent writer on social questions warned the Socialists that when they had got through answering all the rest of their critics, they still had the most difficult one left—Sumner.

Scarcely a single major issue of the present remains untreated in his writings: war, arbitration, governmental extravagance, inflation, the tariff, wages, trades-unions, the status of woman, modern marriage, education; and whatever he touches, he illuminates. He is always provocative in his positiveness; one rejoices over him or is enraged at him, but not indifferent.

I AM not sure just when he gave up his bicycle, but should say that it was not long after he was sixty. He somewhat feared the automobiles, which he referred to as "Hell-vahgens." Then he took up walking. Issuing from his house almost exactly at four o'clock, he would start out along the east side of Whitney Avenue and either keep on out past Lake Whitney or turn into East Rock Park and come out on the Ridge Road. At first he walked steadily until he got home, about six-thirty, covering a good deal of ground. Later on, his distances shortened, though he stayed out for the same length of time, and he was likely to sit for a while on the Park benches. I used to see him on these walks now and then, but thought he wanted to be alone and never offered to go with him. At length, however, Mrs. Sumner told me that he would like a companion but that he would not ask anyone because he thought he went so slowly and so short a distance that it would be boring for a younger man. He was beset by the fear that he might impose trouble on others. So then I sounded him out and, after I had told him that I hated walking as an exercise, though I didn't mind a little of it as a social function, provided it was slow strolling, he said he would always be pleased if I joined him.

I have now a conviction that he wanted companionship, or a breaking of his isolation, more than he allowed himself, in his sensitiveness about being a bore to others, to admit. "I note with great pleasure yr promise to write to me. Do not fail to do it. It will give me great pleasure." "Write me the gossip." I wish I had seen this aspect of our relations more clearly at the time.

The first few times I went with him, I was on crutches or used a cane, having torn a leg muscle on the tennis court. I recall hobbling along with him near the golf links, his pace restrained to mine, and saying that I had never seen the allure of chasing a little ball over acres of ground. He looked at me quizzically and then dropped his eyes significantly to my leg. "You think there's not so much difference between that and this?" I asked. "That's what I was thinking," he replied, as we plodded on; "a little ball or a bigger one." Presently: "We've all got to be patient with each other."

In his later years, walking and novel reading seem to have been Sumner's sole recreations. He is said to have been fond of billiards and whist in younger days, and also an attendant upon concerts and the theater; but, except for several Russian and German plays, I do not recall that he ever mentioned being present at a musical or dramatic performance. That Mrs. Sumner could not go may have explained this renunciation.

As for novel reading, mainly he did that during the summers. He mentioned Mrs. Burnett's *Shuttle* as the sort of story he liked. In his library were many novels in many languages; which leads me to say that probably a good deal of this fiction reading was also foreign language cultivation, as in the case of Sienkiewicz, elsewhere alluded to.

While I am at it, I think I had better reassure those tender souls who have concluded sadly that science dwarfs appreciation of "the best" in life, at least so far as Sumner is concerned. Deriving their melancholy conviction from a misconstruction, probably acquired second-hand, of one of Darwin's characteristically humble remarks about his own failings, certain would-be oracles of culture have consistently warned their acolytes against the coarsening, degrading effect of knowing things with exactitude. Much nobler is it not to know anything as it is, but to flit through existence upon a pearly cloud of emotion.

Charles Darwin was an unbelievably modest and self-depreciating man; in his own eyes, he was a dolt who couldn't write English or think straight without infinite painstaking. The fact is that he took the pains, thought straight, and wrote clearly, if not with distinction. Furthermore, he liked the music which was all about him. Emma Darwin was one of the few English girls who had had lessons from Moscheles and even from Chopin *ipsissimus:* and the Darwin household always harbored a grand piano of the most approved make. Darwin heard a great deal of music all his life; the fact that he could not tell one composition from another is nothing. Many of us, too, who are older could not endure to sit, or stand, through a Wagnerian opera, as we once did. One always regrets the impressionability of youth when it is gone. That is all there is to Darwin's remark. Weismann was a pianist of parts; even a realist like Il Duce, along with Einstein, plays the violin. The pretended correlation between science and spiritual decay is nonsense; the true correlation is rather between science and humility. The scientist of parts is unlikely to be a *poseur*—which cannot be said of the professional æsthete.

Mrs. Sumner was something of a musician; her piano stood open at all times. Shortly before his last illness, Sumner remarked upon the beauty of the church music he knew so well: "That's a lovely hymn they sang this morning, 'Bread of the World'; I've heard it all my life." He may not have known just what some overrated *précieux* was doing upon January 10, 1750, at two in the afternoon, but he was acquainted with his poets, and not the English ones alone. The Bible and Shakespeare were at his tongue's end. He might have been the poet he once thought he wanted to be— only his poetry would have been of the type one lives by. Late in life, he read the whole body of Greek tragedy, ostensibly to gather the sociological materials in it; but his comments on the *Agamemnon,* the *Œdipus* trio, and the *Medea* were, apart from their evidence as to the society of their time, and even though read in translation, worthy of the attention of even the *littérateur*.

Even in his high school days, Sumner was in demand as an actor in amateur theatricals. Later on, this aspect of his occasionally and surprisingly broke out. I have said that he was naturally dramatic. During his middle age, he was requested by a group of young women in New Haven to give them his elementary course in political economy. He did so for several years. At the end of each year, he would treat his young ladies to a picnic in the country. On one occasion, the celebration, taking place near Lake Saltonstall, was interrupted by rain. Sumner requisitioned an empty barn and suggested, to while the time away, that they enact Romeo and Juliet, remembering what passages they could. He, it seems, recalled more than anyone else; and the rôle he assumed, languishing over a cart tail, was no less than that of Juliet.

THESE walks of ours extended over many months and ceased only with his final illness. I sometimes think that I derived more education out of them than out of any other hours of my life. And I was not the only one who thus profited. One afternoon, Sumner stopped at the gate of a friend of mine, as he often did on his way to the Park, to say a word to the children; then walked slowly on down the sidewalk. Presently a little gray-haired priest came along and, having noticed Sumner's pause, stopped and asked my friend who the old gentleman might be. "For some time," he explained, "I have seen him on my walks, and we have sat together, two old fellows, on a Park bench and talked. He is the wisest man I ever knew. I have got to taking some of my perplexities to him. He seems to know more about my church than I do myself. Who is he, please?" "That's Professor Sumner," was the reply. "Oh, so that's the explanation! That's it!" exclaimed the priest. "It's Sumner, the great freetrader! I've read a lot of his writing, but I never knew him. The brothers at home will be mightily interested when I tell them." And he set out in Sumner's wake.

I suppose a good many younger men have felt like this father, for Sumner was a master at untangling one's snarls. As usual, he went straight to the core of the difficulty, and he generally made some wise suggestion. During the years following his death there were many occasions when it seemed to me that I sorely needed him to pull me out of some mud-hole in which I was floundering.

Of course I did not get out of this relationship nearly all that I might. I was too young. I realized that there was plenty of treasure there, and I tried to appropriate all I could; but I feel that if I had the chance now, twenty-five years later, I could emerge with many times what I got. There are issues belonging to one's fifties which are, in the thirties, still below the horizon. One reads after some master, wise in experience, like Goethe; and for each decade of living there is the suggestion, admonition, consolation of him who has gone that way before. A keen-minded and high-souled leader has been over all this ground ahead of you, and the conviction is strong that he can be trusted to provide enlightenment for the latter years as for the earlier. I should like to have considered with Sumner some of the aspects of life that appear in middle age and beyond. If there be a future life in some Elysium, I shall hasten to find him where he paces the asphodel meadow and learn how better I could have kept the faith.

Naturally, matters connected with teaching came up between us, over and over. He himself had begun, he said, by taking counsel of and imitating an older colleague, Dexter, and had gradually struck out on his own. The idea of his imitating Mr. Dexter, or anyone else, always amused me. "Every teacher," he writes, "flounders over treacherous ground for some years. Do not get caught. That is all." Of altering a course he said that if a man had his offering going pretty well, he'd better look out how he changed it very much; that one often got it better the first time than later. "It is not possible to humbug the students much but, if you know that, in part, you have only a special cram, they do not. I have always found that it was easier to make an impression with a special cram than with a big broad stock of information."

He said he never knew the names of his students well, and I told him that a prominent man named Shevlin had been discomposed when he inquired as to his mark—always a good one—because Sumner did not know his name. Sumner asked: "Who is this 'Sheldon,' anyhow?" I told him. He went on a few steps, then inquired if I had ever heard of an athlete named Stagg. I said I had. "Pretty prominent fellow, wasn't he? Thought so. Well, once I called him up to recite and while he was on his feet, I forgot his name. I often did that. So I asked, when I got through with him: 'Name?' and the whole class seemed to be a little shocked." In a faculty meeting, along in the early 1900's, there was much discussion over football. Sumner sat silent until the Dean asked him his opinion. He began: "The last football game I attended was on Thanksgiving Day, eighteen-seventy-six. I don't know anything about it." A piping voice later suggested: "Perhaps Professor Sumner can tell us what Mr. Walter Camp [who was Sumner's brother-in-law] thinks about this." Sumner swung half around. "What do I know about what Camp thinks? Get him in here and he'll tell you. He can say plainly what he thinks, and isn't afraid to."

One evening some of us went down to the old Grand Opera House to see Bob Fitzsimmons in a play containing a representation of a prize fight. The next day I mentioned it to Sumner. "I was there," he stated. "I always thought I'd like to see a real fight and this was the nearest to it that I was likely to get."

The question was once up between us as to the title a prospective assistant professor in the department, who taught mainly human geography, so called, was to have when promoted. "Call him assistant professor of the Science of Society," Sumner decided, promptly. "That's vague enough. And then he can teach anything he likes and no questions asked." Concerning this same young man, who had had an offer from a smaller college and modestly thought he had better take it, as the best he could hope for: "Tell him there's no position here to which he may not aspire. He's a devilish good fellow." Of an uncouth graduate student: "His head's all right, but he lacks acquaintance with the bath (bahth)." To a graduate who had written a highly mathematical thesis, for the publication of which Sumner had "begged" funds: "Now the man who gave this money would like to know just what he's giving it for. I have a certain idea about that, but not much. You try to say, in a few simple words, what you think you've been about, here. I'd like to see such a statement myself." Of "begging" money: "I can always beg a few hundred dollars if it's needed, but I don't want to do it often. I don't want my friends to say: 'There's old Bill Sumner. He'll stick you for some money. Let's dodge around this corner!' " Of a colleague: "He's a good fellow— a devilish good fellow; but he won't fight—he always runs when there's a shindy up." A colleague once joined and accompanied us for several blocks, then put his hand on Sumner's shoulder and remarked, as he turned to leave us: "Well, Yale has *some* great teachers, anyway!" Sumner went on a moment in silence, then looked over his shoulder toward the disappearing gentleman, leaned toward me, and said, in a tone of deep disgust: "He's a gusher!" Of another man: "He was a smart-aleck when he was young, and now he's grown up to be a complete jackahss." I said that somebody we both knew was a fool. "No," Sumner corrected, "he isn't a fool. He's an ahss. You mustn't confuse the two."

We spoke of the amount of time spent by faculties on matters, such as cases of petty discipline, that could be settled by a dean in his office. Sumner said he once amused himself, while the rest were arguing back and forth over an insignificant case, by computing the cost of such a discussion. "I estimated about what each man there was getting per hour's work. When they were done, I said: 'Perhaps the gentlemen would like to know how much it has cost to settle this case.' I think it came to some sixty-odd dollars and some cents. They laughed at themselves, but they'll do it over again the first chance they get."

HE frequently mentioned his conviction that his first job was his teaching—"what I'm paid for"; and used to say that the amount of compensation didn't figure in this. "If a fellow thinks he's paid too little, let him get out and try something else." I said it wasn't so easy to do that. "No. That's so. Especially as you get older, or if you've so identified yourself with a place that the other places think it's no use to call you. Harper tried hard, but he couldn't get anybody from here to go out West with him" (the reference is to President Harper, when he was starting the University of Chicago). He spoke of professors' salaries: "You'll be getting twice what we get now, after a while. It can't be otherwise. But," he added, "the way things look ahead, it may not buy any more for you than ours does for us." He told of a conversation with William C. Whitney, a lifelong friend of his. "Bill said to me: 'Bill, did you ever get a raise?' and I said I had had one, along back. 'How much?' he asked. 'Two hundred and fifty,' I replied. And Bill laughed as if he were at a nigger show." Sumner never got over four thousand dollars, and that only for his last few years; I suppose he referred to the raise from thirty-five hundred which took place in the nineties.

This sum, he said, was not an insufficient one for its period, and he and his wife had not been dependent solely upon it. He said they always had to be careful but were never pinched. I take it he could not have financed his two years of convalescence from his breakdown in Europe. He had not been obliged, however, to work his way through college, and thought it a pity to have to do that. But he hated waste and resented being "held up," not only by the customs officials but also by his employees. One day, he said, he had had to go into the kitchen and settle matters. The maids had been "pestering" Mrs. Sumner about a raise of wages. "So I went out there, and I said: 'Now, I want you to quit this buzzing. I don't want to do it, and I oughtn't to have to, but I'll pay you what you ask. Only don't let me hear any more buzzing.' Of course they were sweet after that and promised everything." These servants were fond of Sumner and devoted to him in his crippled condition. He acknowledged their helpfulness but was unhappy because he needed aid. It was a great triumph when he could manage his own "self-bath."

After his retirement, he said that if he had had daughters, he would feel that he must go on trying to earn money; as it was, it didn't matter. I said one day that I didn't see why anyone needed more than a certain moderate sum annually; that I had never hankered after a private yacht. "I have," he rejoined promptly. "What for?" I asked. "Oh, I'd like to take my friends a ride and give them a good time. It must be fine to do that."

I once heard someone in authority say that Sumner (he was then in his sixties) really had a short schedule of teaching, implying that he did not deserve what some others were getting. I was infuriated, knowing as I did the heavy schedules he had carried through all those years when he was spending his vitality prodigally in a service, unsparing of himself, that made Yale worth while as it would not have been without him. To many a man, Sumner was about all there was to Yale. There are always jackals to yelp about the aging or dead lion.

Mrs. Sumner once told me that when they came to New Haven her husband decided that they would have to set aside two hundred dollars a year for books, however much that might cramp them in other respects. He was much amused, she said, at her idea that it would be nice to have a horse and carriage. He always put his duty to the College ahead of everything else, she said. This extended to refusal to make engagements that involved cutting his classes; he made the most strenuous effort to be present every time—"to be where I ought to be." One blizzardy winter day when the street cars were not yet running, some of us graduate students were curious as to whether Sumner, then not so strong, had been stopped. We went over to see, and while we were looking into A-1 Osborn, he tramped in, very red and puffing, with high leather boots over his trousers and a look of triumph on his face. He had risen very early and tramped in through the drifts, to arrive fifteen minutes before his class, as usual.

Upon the last day of the year 1907, I think it was, he suffered a stroke that crippled his right hand and used him up considerably otherwise. While he was brushing his teeth, the brush had fallen from his hand, which was useless thereafter for months. I shall return later on to this period. For some weeks he could not attend his classes, and I used to go to his house to get the questions for them. He always had them ready, and they were long and involved. Finally, when it was decided that he was well enough to start again, he asked me to come down to see him through if he needed me. We took a cab at his house and started off for Osborn Hall. All the way down he seemed to be mounting in eagerness and satisfaction. He smelt the battle again, as he neared the field. We got out on College Street and I helped him up the outer steps and then to the second floor. He climbed very slowly and puffed a good deal, but his spirits seemed to be rising all the time. When he had seated himself at his desk, after I had helped him remove his overshoes and overcoat, he grinned to me and said: "This is better!" I urged him not to overdo—he had two classes in succession—and promised to look in at the end of the first hour. When I arrived, he was still going strong, and kept the class five minutes over time. The succeeding hour he did the same thing, and when I went in to help him to the cab, he grunted: "Not dead yet!" He was very cheerful all the way home and thereafter would not hear of my accompanying him, though for several successive times I met him and saw that he got upstairs safely. He set promptly to work to learn to write with his left hand, which he did not do very well; the other hand was in a sling for a long time, and for months he used to rub it with the left as if to restore circulation.

He was sympathetic, somewhat banteringly, with my impatience of the drawbacks to the profession. "It's like taking a vow of poverty," he admitted, "but it has its compensations. One of them is intellectual freedom. Despite all my troubles, I have always been able to say out what I thought. We have always had freedom of speech here." Once, when I expressed disillusionment, he said, severely: "That's all true; but you're too young to know it." He never cherished any illusions as to the influence he had exerted—in fact, he much underestimated it and everything else he had done— nor do I recall any mention of influence upon the young as one of the opportunities of the profession. If he thought of that at all, I think it was as of a by-product—the essential being the relentless pursuit of truth and the pitiless exposure of fraud and pretense.

In the dedication of a book to Sumner, a youthful author used several lines based on Homer:

> With strong hand thou layest open the gates of the mind.
> To hate the false and to charge upon it with relentless spirit
> We younger men have learned from thee. To thee be thanks.

Sumner said he had got out his lexicon and read the lines. "Very handsome of you; I like it." When the dedication was submitted to Professor T. D. Seymour, to be sure it was correct, he said: "I am very glad you're dedicating your book to Mr. Sumner; and that νηλέϊ θυμῷ is just right for him. 'With relentless spirit'; that's exactly the way he goes at it."

I think he believed that his task was to sow and water, and that "the Lord giveth the increase"—if there was to be any. Anyway, he never wasted time counting hypothetical sheaves.

A good many men yet living can bear witness to his readiness to labor painstakingly in helping them with difficulties which they had referred, in post-college years, to him. I believe there is plenty of evidence that, no matter how busy he was, or how ill, he honored all such calls upon him. His letters were always brief as he could make them, but they were not careless or evasive. The answers were adequate.

One summer, after his hand was lamed, he received a letter asking, as I recall it, about that portion of the surplus revenue of 1837 that fell to a certain small town in Connecticut. He passed the letter over to me, as we walked from the Fisher's Island post office. It seemed to me hopelessly intricate and detailed in its query. "That can't be answered offhand," I said. "It takes a good deal of nerve to put a question like that to a man, especially during vacation." "Well," he replied, "I can answer it," and he began a detailed explanation which covered the query completely, so far as I could see. I was astonished and said so. How could he recall all that, and how had he dug it up in the first place? "Years ago," said he, "I had Edward Bourne look all that up for his dissertation, and so I remember it. But I can't write it out for this man, with this hand." "I will do that," I volunteered, "if you will dictate it." When we got back, he sat down and condensed what he had said into a page or so, and the letter went off that day.

I wish here to reproduce the kind of letter Sumner wrote to inquiring ex-students.

"I never had many close friends on the faculty," said Sumner once. "There's nobody now except Edward Dana. He and I used to spend a lot of time together, evenings, going over the course of study and batting at moths that flew in the windows, hot summer nights. Most of my old friends are in New York." I recall his sober face when he told me that he must attend "that funeral [William C. Whitney's] in New York."

"Well, we've put Greek on the top shelf, along with Hebrew," he announced, one day. "I can't believe it!" I replied. "No, I don't wonder. But it's so, all the same; the incredible sometimes happens. Greek won't be a required subject any more. After a while we'll get philosophy up there too. No subject ought to be required, as better and nobler than all the rest."

I SUPPOSE," I ventured once, early in our acquaintance, "that I ought to go over and study in Germany." "Why so?" he countered. "Everyone seems to think so, and tell me so." "That's nonsense!" he retorted, impatiently. "You know how to read German, and I can teach you all the sociology there is." And he went on to express a low opinion of German scholarship in his line, except for Lippert, Gumplowicz, and Ratzenhofer. "If you ever see anything you think is important, in German, translate it into English and see if it is. The German language lends itself easily to bathos." He added that he owed a good deal to the Germans with whom he studied theology; that "those men in Göttingen" gave him his first impetus to go to the facts fearlessly, regardless of orthodox tradition. Later, I mentioned to him that one professor told me he wouldn't vote for a man as professor who hadn't studied in Germany, and he sneered at such an "exhibition of fetishism."

Spencer, he said, gave him his start in social science; that he was a great analytic mind. I said that his autobiography seemed to reveal him as a kind of old maid. "That's exactly what he was," Sumner confirmed. "We entertained him when he came over here. An old maid from the word go." I remarked how different Darwin was. "Yes," said Sumner, "he was a man, a great and good one. I must read that Life of him by his son again pretty soon." And then he adverted, as he did several other times, to an apparently mistaken observation of Darwin about the Fuegians. "If we can't trust Mr. Darwin, who is there to trust? But I suppose everyone must make mistakes, and he made mighty few." He then told me about how certain alumni in Buffalo had asked President Porter, who had just addressed them, about "Marsh's horses," concerning which all his hearers were then curious and excited, and that the reverend gentleman had said: "Oh, they aren't anything. Only a few old bones in a box." This, Sumner conceived, was an illustration of how a man, by always fixing his mind upon "moral philosophy," could lose perception of the line of demarkation between truth and falsehood. One of his favorite stories was about Dr. Porter's horror over John Tyndall's proposed scientific test of prayer—where Tyndall suggested praying for the patients in one wing of a hospital and not in another, and comparing the death rate. "Porter," Sumner said, "nearly stood on his head with rage, and finally calmed down to the statement that Mr. Tyndall did not know what prayer was."

A companion-piece to his puzzlement over Darwin's error was his inability to understand Mr. Cleveland's Venezuela message. I think he blamed it to the influence of Olney.

It happened that February 12, 1909, fell upon the day of the week when the Anthropology Club regularly met. As I went down with Sumner, I spoke of this being Darwin's, and also Lincoln's, centenary, and he marveled at the fact that "they were twins." In introducing the speaker that night, he made reference to Darwin and called upon us to honor him, "for we must all remember what Mr. Darwin has done for us."

This Anthropology Club was a kind of pet—a late-born child— of Sumner's. He regularly led off the year with a paper of some kind and was always present. One year his paper was on "Evolution in the Superorganic Domain"—really Evolution in the Mores. He took the position that there was no such thing. The meeting was large, and a good many men opposed his view. He fought back with his usual force and skill and, in the end, it was decided to let all the objectors have a say. There was a series of papers by Barrell, Judd, Day, and others, the net result of which amounted to a criticism of Sumner's use of the word "evolution" as synonymous with "progress," whereas it meant merely "adjustment." Sumner had a good many passages from Darwin to back up his contention that evolution was progressive, but was evidently somewhat shaken; for, as we walked home the last evening of the controversy, he told me, after silent meditation for some blocks: "I guess I'll leave that chapter out of *Folkways*." Perhaps this paper should be published under the title "Progress and the Mores," for it is a severe arraignment, reminiscent of his most pungent controversial utterances, of the easy optimist. Sumner saw no progress—in his conception, therefore, no evolution—except in the organization for society's self-maintenance, and especially in mechanical inventions. Otherwise the mores were "a tumbling sea of clouds." As the manuscript stands I have felt that he was right in holding it back. He simply dropped it and went on to complete *Folkways* without it. Then he was much wearied, became ill, and, so far as I know, never returned to the subject.

This is one of the cases which convince me that, with all his effort to "cram up a knowledge of science," Sumner never succeeded in fully emancipating himself from his early training. Nevertheless, the change he wrought in himself and his trend of thought by turning away from his theological training toward science, is perhaps his greatest achievement; in any case, it rendered *Folkways* and *The Science of Society* possible. He remained at his best, however, in the brief exposition of his convictions concerning contemporary issues. The short, attacking essay was his forte. I have often thought, and others have arrived at the same conclusion, that he was primarily and naturally a preacher of righteousness, though not so much an exhorter as a denouncer of unrighteousness. I am offering nothing in derogation of such books as his biographies of Hamilton, Jackson, and Morris—least of all of *Folkways*, which I regard as a classic *tour de force;* but for sheer power and brilliance I do not think they compare with *What Social Classes Owe to Each Other,* or *Protectionism,* or his series of essays on Liberty, or such more isolated efforts as "The Absurd Effort to Make the World Over," or "The Examination of a Noble Sentiment." *Folkways,* except for the first chapters, reveals the writer as aged and weary. Though significant for general enlightenment far beyond anything else he did, it succeeds by reason of its deep insight and massive evidence, rather than because of its style, form, or arrangement. Compared with the essays that ran like hot, impetuous metal from the crucible (he told me that, in younger days, he could never write fast enough to keep up with his thought), *Folkways* is hard, unexciting reading; and his manuscript fragments on *The Science of Society* were not dissimilar. They were, naturally, a first draft; but they amounted, for the most part, to a series of transcribed, not always translated, notes, strung along upon a thin and discontinuous thread. There was not much connective tissue. The binding element lay in his system of classification and in his head; just what his own hand would have eventually constructed, no one can ever say. Of a brief manuscript based upon a small section of his collections and submitted by me to him during his last months of life, he told his wife that he had not supposed anyone else would have written up the matter concerned so nearly as he himself would have done. Those familiar with Sumner's inimitable ways of saying things will detect passages, here and there, in *The Science of Society* that remain exactly as he wrote them. They stand out like streaks of quartz. But the general exposition is another's.

I may recall, in this connection, one curiously impractical method practiced by Sumner. When it came to the index of *Folkways,* he used a number of heavy, expensive ledgers. He guessed at the space needed for his entries and laboriously paged back and forth. I heard him tell the president of a large public service corporation how he was doing it, and the listener suggested tentatively that some kind of a card catalogue would be handier. "It might," replied Sumner, "but I've got to doing it the way I told you." When the index was done, he tore off the covers of his ledgers, tied their mutilated viscera together, and sent the huge bundle along, not without misgivings as to its safety—he had carried the manuscript of *Folkways* to the Boston publishers by hand. In this case, the publisher, Sumner told me, returned the package with the comment, politely phrased, that what he wanted was "an index, not a concordance." Sumner chuckled a little over that, rather ruefully; then set to work cutting out the product of hours of labor until he had reduced the mass to manageability.

THE impression made by Sumner's essays upon students has been truly astonishing. There was a futile sort of committee appointed, several years after Sumner's death, to formulate a list of reading for a proposed variation on the M.A. degree—a list which should cover the best in general literature, as a kind of exhaustive background of culture. It was a foolish task, very likely; at any rate, it came to nothing; but the committee was a good one, under the chairmanship of Dean Cross, the present Governor of Connecticut. We sat around, making suggestions and getting them accepted or turned down. It was agreed that no works under fifty years old should be proposed. At length, however, one of the committee—not the present writer—said that he would like to break the fifty-year rule and advocate the inclusion of Sumner's essays; that he had observed for some years their enlivening effect upon classes in the Scientific School and could not allow them to go unproposed in such a course of reading as we were trying to assemble. General assent was at once forthcoming. This was the only exception to the rule.

There is no doubt, in my own experience, for it was in my courses that the essays were read, as to this gentleman's judgment; and in this connection I can recount what has seemed to me a strange and even startling phenomenon. For the last twenty-odd years, since Sumner's death, I have seen graduate students under his spell, experiencing a sense of personal touch, much as if he were present in the flesh. They have acted as if they had known him and have themselves remarked that they felt they did know him. What they certainly have acquired, chiefly from his vivid essays, is a perception of personality as impressed upon the written word so strong that, as some of them have expressed it, Sumner's shade has seemed to be present in its former intellectual haunts. And, along with the conviction that they were personally acquainted with him, have invariably gone that respect and even reverence which many of us older men felt for him during his life with us. I know of no similar case; and this one is all but uncanny.

Every year, of course, I have had our graduate students see and handle the materials Sumner left to me; and I have noted in them, in the presence of his imposing *reliquia,* the same initial discouragement and eventual stimulation that I myself felt, long before them. As an asset to his successors, Sumner does not wear out, or even wear thin. The best of him cannot become antiquated because it is the fruit of insight—and by that I do not mean intuition but understanding wrought out by hard work—into things and processes which are permanent features in the life of society.

Returning for a moment to Sumner's outlook on science—once, when there was given, in the Anthropology Club, a brief sketch of Weismannism, Sumner asked the speaker: "Can you really *believe* that those sub-microscopic ids and determinants are actually living things? I can't conceive of it, myself." "But if there are any subdivisions of the chromosomes that carry heredity, they must be alive; and the chromosome as an undivided whole doesn't account for what we see." "I know it," Sumner admitted, "but I can't conceive of those little things being alive, anyhow."

Sumner was a good deal influenced in his estimation of a writer's work by his impression of the author as a man. Of one rather bruited book, though it was second-rate and has not lasted, Sumner said he didn't care to read it because the author was of a detestable character. He admired Darwin all the more, as a scientist, by reason of the quality of his private life, and I recall his pleasure at learning that Julius Lippert was something the same sort of man. Concerning a writer or, for that matter, any person who lived self-respectingly and honorably under handicaps of poverty or ill fortune, as Lippert did, he used to comment: "The suffering righteous!"

I do not mean to say that Sumner neglected real contributions to knowledge, even from a scurvy knave; but he seemed to read and to quote such an author with a kind of disdain and distrust. On the other hand, he hated to criticize a good man. Of Ripley's *Races of Europe* he wrote: "I must say that the results seemed to me *very uncertain.* I am very skeptical about the data and also about

craniology in general. I wd not say this in public for that book
cost great labor. I fear that it was largely wasted."

However tartly Sumner jibed at ethics as a study, he stood for
morality at all times, in season and, as some would doubtless say,
out of season. I have no doubt that he would have been much better
pleased if Goethe had "behaved himself," despite the facts that, as
he knew, the poet had not departed very widely from the mores of
his time, place, and class, and had made acknowledgment to convention both by marrying the mother of his children and by warning others against the course he had himself pursued.

WHAT impressed me most, perhaps, as I came to know
Sumner better, was that he seldom or never lapsed into
vacancy of mind; nor, I might add, did he repeat himself,
old-man-fashion, during even his last years. He seemed always to
be revolving various matters of serious import, even when ostensibly seeking recreation. His mind was always at a tension. He
used to carry in a wallet small slips of paper, cut for the purpose,
upon which he would jot down his reflections; then he would cram
them into his trousers pocket. I have seen him dig into that pocket
and come out with a handful of crumpled memoranda, a number of
which turned up later in his note files and were of considerable use
in various connections. They were really notes to himself, joggings
to memory, generally connected with the subject upon which he
was engaged or aspects of things that suggested themselves to
him for treatment. He left a sizable blank book, labeled "SUB-
JECTS," containing several hundred titles for prospective essays
or books, with an indication as to lines of development. These look
as if they had taken origin from his slips and are highly sugges-
tive. Some of them, notably a series on Democracy and Plutoc-
racy, were written up in essay form; I quote a few of the many
that were not.

Novels as Agents of Uniformity of Ideas throughout a Culture Area.
Nineteenth Century Superstitions.
  Myth making (find'g democ. & modern ideas in village comm. & prim.
  times) god-making (fads, coop.) Myth: banquet of life; simplicity of
  M.A. Brentano Trades Unions. Gilds. Press. Education. The Good
  New Times coming. Social compact. Equality.

Metapolitics.

Don Quixote's Political Economy.

The Moral Right of the Man who has met all the regular demands of the Society on him to Peace and Quiet.

Learned Men of the M.A.

Abelard Gershon Aquinas Scotus Gerbert.

Albertus Magnus.

What was a scholar? Fortunes and fate.

Whether Christianity in the Middle Ages, but for the Papacy, would have frittered away into Sects?

Nature & Limits of Superstition.

Is there a boundary between superstition and non-superstitious faith in the absolute and universal.

Rum and Aborigines.

Goitre.

History of Patriotism.

What it was in Greece, Rome, M.A. What it is in Modern State. The Us-Group. Nationality, Nationalism. Allegiance. In Church. "Church steeple patriotism." American notion of it.

It is argued in bar of the broad free trade doctrine that it is essential for a State to have a peasant (or agricultural) class in it and that it is therefore expedient to put protective taxes on grain in order to preserve such a class.

Is any class essential to a state? What would be the operation of an enactment which should rob a state of an essential class? What would happen to a state which should lose a class essential to its existence? Seek examples of states which had no peasant class. Is there a misconception of human society in this argument?

Games of Chance and the Gambling Appetite.

The Moral Effect of Changing a Crucifix into a Cross.

Effect of M.A. realism about crucifixion, tortures of martyrs, etc. on imagination, love of cruelty, treatment of enemies and heretics. Carnality. Effect of abandoning this, or causes of it.

What are the Parasites of Human Society?

Idle rich? Criminals? pseudo and real defective, dependent and delinquent? adventurers? gamblers? speculators? profession and literary classes? monks and nuns? police, army, navy, civil servants?

The Blessing or the Curse of Being Rational Beings.

We can study our own case. We try to better it. Penalty of error and error unavoidable. Oldest social reflexion is about beggars and vagrants. Not solved.

The Penalties of Progress.
    Destroys vested interests and achievements. Long vs. short interest.
    Routine. "The Better is the enemy of the Good."
Salt.

Another use of Sumner's slips was to record words in foreign
languages which he had failed to find in his own dictionaries. When
he had gathered a number of them, he used to repair to some
library, often in connection with his trips to New York, and look
them up. Then he punctiliously entered them in his dictionaries at
home.

Thus he kept incessantly upon the trail, always turning over in
his mind some question or other that he had put to himself or that
was suggested by what he saw. "Freudvoll, leidvoll, gedankenvoll
sein": he had his joys, and a good many sorrows; but he was
always reflecting, weighing, arriving at judgments that seemed
almost extemporaneous but were not. It was hard to catch him un-
prepared, without a reasoned opinion. And this witnesses to his
wide intellectual curiosity. However, it would be incorrect to compare him with so many-sided a type as Goethe. Sumner was a very
serious man. Living in the world seemed to him a highly momentous
business. I think he was predisposed, in his interest and thought,
toward the weightier issues of individual and social existence; he
had concentrated, early in life, upon religious and moral matters,
and preoccupation with them had rather submerged the lighter
interests. Moral issues were always, it seems to me, uppermost in
his mind. He had a great pity for human woes and strove single-
mindedly to learn how to alleviate them.

He labored unceasingly to find the laws of the inevitable, with
the idea of teaching men to recognize and adjust to them. Having
attained what he believed to be the truth, he announced it im-
placably. If men would insist upon defying Nature, they would end
up in the gutter, like the drunkard. You did not find the temperate
and self-controlled in that predicament, for they had faced the
realities and submitted to them. They had practiced self-denial
and self-discipline. They were the fit; their interests should never
be forgotten; and it was a pity, and unfair, and also dangerous to
society's life, that they should have to subtract from their own

and their children's self-realization to prop up empty sacks that could not stand alone. Said one of his colleagues, after his death: "I've been reading over Sumner's *Social Classes.* I used to think it was hard doctrine. It is, but, confound it! it's *true!*"

No one who knew Sumner personally could imagine that he liked hard doctrine for its own sake. He would gladly have believed in all the yearning optimism and "creative" and "constructive" thinking there was, if he could have done so. Who wouldn't? But he knew what has happened in the past, whenever mankind had followed a will-o'-the-wisp, and he set his face sternly against fantasy-spinning. To conclude, however, from his uncompromising bluntness that Sumner was a cold, unsympathetic soul, is to judge as a fool. He faced things as they are, in all their unperfectibility. He would have been the first to lift the drunkard out of the gutter. The sot was where he belonged, but he couldn't be left there. Sumner once wrote of lynching: "The badness of the victim is not an element in the case at all. Torture and burning are forbidden, not because the victim is not bad enough, but because we are too good. It is on account of what we owe to ourselves that these methods are shameful to us, if we descend to them."

During Sumner's last illness, while he was in a New Jersey hospital, I had occasion to go to his house in New Haven. I was admitted by an elderly woman who was acting as caretaker. She asked me, in a pronounced brogue, how Mr. Sumner was. My report was not encouraging, and she began to cry. It seems that she had been a housemaid in the family years before, had married and soon lost her husband; and that Sumner had looked after her interests, seen to her boys' education, and found them their chance in life. What the mother thought of Sumner was evident enough; and she told me, too, and eloquently. I suppose that he would have been embarrassed to the point of rage if he had ever been found out and faced with his secret deeds of helpfulness. There must have been a good many other cases; he told me that after he retired he would have to "cut down on a lot of these small contributions to this and that," or he couldn't live on his half pay.

My impression of Sumner is that of a wise and farseeing man who, perceiving even in his earlier years the tragedy of human existence, viewed it with a kind of despair and with a wincing distress. It hurt him to see it; and he threw himself into a lifetime's effort, along the only lines that seemed to him to promise results in the way of alleviation. He castigated human follies with a vigor and severity that were a measure of his recognition of the sufferings they entailed. He assaulted false leaders, especially the ones whom he regarded as deliberate batteners upon human weaknesses, with inexorable wrath. He defended with fervor the "suffering righteous," as they struggled along under the cynical impositions put upon them. It deeply offended him that A and B, self-righteous uplifters, should put their heads together and decide what C, the "Forgotten Man," should do for D, the wastrel. His eye was always upon C, of whom he was a fervent admirer and a passionate partisan. A and B were invited by him to mind their own business so far as C was concerned; let them do for D themselves if they liked, but let them quit imposing upon C.

What do social classes owe to each other? *"To increase, multiply, and extend the chances."* Plans to rob one in order to give to another "nourish some of the meanest vices of human nature, waste capital, and overthrow civilization. But if we can expand the chances [through improvement in education, science, art, or government] we can count on a general and steady growth of civilization and advancement of society by and through its best members. In the prosecution of these chances we all owe to each other good will, mutual respect, and mutual guarantees of liberty and security. Beyond this nothing can be affirmed as a duty of one group to another in a free state."

Naturally, Sumner's uncompromising position in the statement of such principles drew upon him the abuse of many less disinterested persons; and there have been a number of high-minded people who, not themselves very profound, looked upon him with hostility. To one of Sumner's colleagues Theodore Roosevelt said that he did not like Sumner; he liked everyone else he knew on the Yale and Harvard faculties—all but Charles Eliot Norton and Sumner. "They both lie." It might be interpolated that Sumner's opinion of Roosevelt was a far from flattering one. It too centered about veracity. "We shall all have to vote for Teddy in 1908," he writes, in 1906, "in order to ward off Bryan and Hades. If I do it (vote for Teddy) I shall be disgraced forever." But a good many of us have loved Sumner, as many loved Roosevelt, for the enemies he made. He was a strong hater and a strong lover, as must happen where the essence of a man's character is strength.

I take it to be the plain fact, that Sumner always presented a dual aspect, one which was favorable to misunderstanding and misrepresentation. In his public utterances he stated the exact truth as he saw it, recking not at all that it was sure to be unpalatable to many. Such-and-such conditions in society were inexpedient, wrong, and sure to promote, not to lessen, the woes of humanity; the true course to be followed was thus-and-so, if men were to evade collision with inevitabilities. These conclusions were stated vigorously, even harshly—indeed, with the ruthlessness of the sensitive spirit that feels obliged to enforce a sad truth. But when it came to his private life, Summer faced things as they were, in all their imperfection and inadequacy, and hastened to relieve, as he could, such cases of misery as he encountered. In theory, there was to him nothing promising at all except rational action in the light of science; in practice (not in the long run but in the short, not in accord with the long interest but with the short and immediate one), a hand must be extended to the victims of the system, vicious though that succor might turn out to be. "We have all got to be patient with each other."

Perhaps the dominant trait in Sumner was his fidelity to duty. Nowhere does this come out more clearly than in his college connections. When he wrote his letter to his colleagues setting forth the attempted interference with his work on the part of the administration, he stated: "I have always considered that the Corporation did me great honor when they elected me, a young and untried man, to this important chair. I have tried to justify their confidence. I threw myself into the work of my department and of the college with all my might. I had no other interest or ambition. I have refused (until within six months) to entertain any proposition to go away or to go into other work." And when it turned out that Sumner was not to be interfered with and dictated to, he resumed his labors with renewed vigor and loyalty. If, within the institution, there developed untoward situations, though they touched his personal interest in no direct manner, he did not spare himself in his efforts to oppose and rectify them, for he saw the university as a whole and education as an issue not to be approached from one angle alone, much less from the direction of private or departmental advantage.

He used to say that Yale must have great vitality to have stood all that she had had to stand, and that she "had profited greatly by her losses"; that what she needed was a few more first-class funerals—"mine among 'em. We all get old and casehardened and ought to pass on." He was much in favor of establishing an age for retirement and judged sixty-eight to be none too early. Once in a while, he admitted, a man would be useful after that age, but not often. One of the ways of serving the institution was "to walk the plank," to "join Andy Carnegie's kindergarten," betimes. "You younger fellows will do a lot better job than we old ones. You'll read all the books that come out and be able to do a lot more for the students."

IT was the student, the "forgotten student," to whom chiefly Sumner's loyalty was rendered, and when he thought of Yale he had in mind above all, I believe, the undergraduate body, present, past, and to be. "I get my lesson every day just like the boys have to," he said. This was literally true, for he conscientiously reread his assignments, no matter how familiar he was with them from many former readings, on the evenings before his class exercises. On one occasion when he was assisting a debating team, in contrast to other speakers who made their addresses from the floor, he laboriously ascended the platform. "I believe," he began, "in placing myself in the same situation as the student."

I will here complete, while I am at it, the story of a famous evening. The debating team had the negative of the question as to the advisability of setting up a Hague Tribunal. Apparently this side of the issue so appealed to Sumner that he emerged from the retirement imposed upon him by illness and appeared in Osborn Hall, a little late, seating himself in the rear and off to one side. The announced speakers, chief among them a learned and eminent lawyer, Judge Simeon E. Baldwin, made their addresses, to which the debaters listened with close attention, taking down all they could. Judge Baldwin offered a plea for the Tribunal. Then Mr. Hadley, who was presiding, having noticed Sumner's entrance, requested him, if he were able, to say something. Sumner solemnly plodded down the aisle, climbed the steps of the platform rather painfully, refused a chair, and, planting himself in his usual massive way, made the remark about placing himself in the same position as the students. He first attacked "my friend, Judge Baldwin" who, he said, had voiced no more than a "pious hope." The Judge apparently much appreciated this and other "digs," as Sumner used to call them, for his rather austere calm was replaced by evidences of amusement, not all beard-concealed.

Finally Sumner wound up with the following simple proposition: "If people are mad enough, they will fight; if not, the ordinary means of diplomacy will do." The team seized upon this formula and, reiterating it in debate, came off as winners. It is almost unnecessary to say that Sumner was stating exactly what he believed and that part of his impressiveness lay in his depth of conviction. Whether he was right or not is another matter, as it was in his *Conquest of the United States by Spain,* where his conviction was at least equally profound. But, irrespective of whether one agreed with him, there was no question, after he had spoken, about the clearness of the issue. My friends on the debating team said they got from his speech something they could set their teeth in.

Interested as he was in the undergraduate, he had little patience with poor teaching. "He may know a lot, but he can't tell it" was one of his unfavorable characterizations; and he thought that muddiness of exposition was a sign of muddled thinking. "A man like Huxley had no trouble along that line." The issue between "research" and teaching never bothered him at all. I do not recall much use by him of the former term—certainly it was no fetish to him, for he was not taken in by the German godlet, nor did he adorn his sentences with "Seminar," "Semester," "Fach," and the rest of the tin panoply of the strutting academic Lohengrin. Nor did he mistake a goose for a swan, or a swan on wheels for a live bird, even in an operatic setting. At a time when "German" meant something akin to "infallible," he could tell you both the virtues and the defects of German scholarship—and British and French, too—from experience in Europe and with European literatures. He was difficult to impress and always ready to assess notable figures anew. "It's a pity Huxley lost his grip in that *Evolution and Ethics* thing of his." "What did Darwin want to go off into metaphysics for in *The Descent of Man?*" He knew no super-man, and no super-methods.

What has come to be called "Research," and has been, as a fetish, much acclaimed, often by talkers who have themselves done none of it, he referred to merely as "work" or "study." He made fun of the eccentric pomposity of any writer on the order of "Der selige Bastian," who, he said, was reverenced by the Germans mainly because nobody could understand him. Bastian, he said, slipped in Greek and even Hebrew phrases, when they happened to occur to him before the German ones did, and also all sorts of occult allusions, so that no reader could follow him unless his mental outfit exactly superposed upon Bastian's. He thought that this eccentric style was partly due to laziness and partly to the desire to "show off." "Bastian didn't trouble himself about being clear. I guess he knew how to impress his audience." Sumner made no parade of his own studies. He used to say: "I've got a lot of notes but," with a sigh, "the question is what I can do with them." He seemed a little proud of his industry and somewhat astonished at it. His own bibliography, by no means complete, contains over two hundred and fifty items. When someone asked him where he had got the time to do all the study involved in *Folkways*, he replied that he didn't know, that he had just "plugged along" every day, without thinking much about it, and, after a while, there was the stuff. Like Darwin, again, he felt that "it's dogged as does it."

Sumner never thought of minimizing unremitting study as an essential to proper teaching, least of all in a new and unstereotyped subject like his own. He had an unbroken stream of new books and journals passing over his desk. A clergyman once told me he thought maybe he could "stick" Sumner by having read Harnack's big *Dogmengeschichte* shortly after it came out, especially since Sumner no longer read theology; but found that Sumner had completed the volumes some time before. It is sometimes alleged, with pontifical solemnity, generally by some oracle who has done neither the one nor the other well, that research and teaching are incompatible. Sumner, they say, was an exception in being eminent in both lines; but he held no such view about that matter of incompatibility. Far from being detrimental to teaching, diligent and incessant study, according to him, was an indispensable requisite to it. This he took to be axiomatic and spent no time talking about it.

But when it came to teaching, he had no use for the inarticulate or the negligent—least of all for anyone who thought teaching was beneath him. "He'd better learn how to do it before he despises it. Our job is to keep school." He regarded any appointment, however ostentatious, as very dubious if the appointee couldn't "hold up his end in the real work of the place." He abominated the "stuffed shirt." He had about as much enthusiasm for decorative men as for pretentious buildings, being but slightly impressionable by façades of any description. He once anxiously planned a building which he thought he was going to get for the Social Sciences. "Brick's good enough," he told me. "It's the inside I'm thinking about—light, convenience for work, and so on." After his death, a correspondent deplored the simple stone that marks his grave in the Guilford cemetery and called for a monument. I can hear Sumner laugh sardonically at the idea. If he had chosen his own memorial it would have been some such "shop" as the building he long hoped for and never got. For "Prunk," as he called it, in structure or man, made no appeal to him.

In connection with his hoped-for building, Sumner said he had to be very careful about approaching his prospective donor. "He is the sort of man every cell of whose body, when you ask him for something, rises up and bawls 'No!'" Sumner ought to have known, for he himself had no difficulty about saying "No!" One of my colleagues has a story about that. As a student, he had innocently asked Sumner to make a Phi Beta Kappa address. The ensuing explosive negative made him feel, he says, as if his line of retreat were a mile long.

The center of the issue about teaching and research lies, of course, in publication: profound knowledge without any ink-spilling of impressive copiousness—impressive to rival institutions ("See what We are doing!")—is at a discount. But Sumner, while he prized the printed word of a competent and disinterested truth-seeker, did not confuse volubility, vocal or printed, with scholarship. He could recognize investigation that had its long and brooding silences, as compared with the variety that, as someone once put it, "wants its dividends paid monthly." And he recognized green fruit, plucked untimely for marketing purposes—kiln-dried timber—at sight. He knew what seasoning means. He was not for the instant publication of raw doctoral dissertations in quantitarian inter-university rivalry. Let it be recalled that he held his own stuff back because "I prefer to correct my own mistakes."

On the other hand, he felt that when one had studied long and diligently, he had a right, or even a duty, to state his conclusions; and he was much disappointed when Seymour, a lifetime student of Homer, over-conscientiously restricted himself, in the book of his life, to conclusions for which he could give chapter and verse—to the authority of others rather than his own. And he told the author how he felt about it: "I wrote him I had been looking forward to his own views. He ought to have given them. He has the right. Maybe he will, now he has once satisfied his over-scrupulousness."

In the case of younger men who worked at his side, he was always interested in what we found out and, to our pride, took it right up into his own notes; but he never exercised the slightest pressure upon us to publish. We might, by letting up on our studies, have printed a deal of slight, even if popular, stuff without impressing him at all. He was encouraging when we had discovered for ourselves things which he had long known, and only incidentally did he let it come out that he had passed that way before us.

We felt that we were working with, rather than under, him, and that he trusted us. "Keller," he would say to me, "I wish you'd read those books on sociology and tell me what's in them. I haven't time to read any more systematic works now. If I stop to do that, I'll die before I do my own book. Time's short with me."

Regarding longer and shorter writings of all kinds, Sumner had, he said, three questions to ask: *What is it?* (Have you told what you've got, so that we know just what it is?) *How do you know it?* (Where's your evidence?) WHAT OF IT? It seems that a good many learned productions failed, to his mind, to survive the application of that final criterion. Research, however *tief eingehend*, however *gründlich*, that came through with insignificant results (consider, for instance, a learned investigation *Über die Wurzelfestigheit der*

Haupthaare bei Chinesen—"Concerning the Root-firmness of the Head-hair among Chinese") impressed him as little as a flashy exposition of some bright idea, "thought out in bed." What he most admired was the product of persistent labor over verified and reverified facts, issuing in some result bearing upon human living and set forth with utter candor and unadorned clarity. And, so far as teaching went, I think he, as one responsible for the destiny of Yale College, would always have voted for the man who could transmit ideas to the students, even though that man were incapable of making discoveries of his own, rather than for the inarticulate scholar who lacked the power of opening minds by awakening interest.

I do not know just what the late Professor Giddings meant by the following expression, unless it is a tribute to Sumner's engrossment in pure science and his refusal to run off into whims and side issues: "William Graham Sumner whom, now that he is gone, we are beginning to recognize as perhaps the most consistently sociological if not the greatest of sociologists." I myself think Sumner the foremost student of the science of society who has yet lived. I think him much better informed and much sounder than Spencer, his nearest rival. It is needless to say, to anyone who knew his humble estimate of his own doings, that he harbored no such sentiment about himself.

IV

MANY a man, I dare say, looks back at his earlier years with incredulity, not being able to believe that he has been as foolish as he knows he was; to him, older now and enlightened by experience, it even seems that his youth must have been spotted by periods of genuine mental unbalance. Sumner was always tolerant of such vagaries, perhaps because he could recall his own; he said, one time, that he could not understand why he had been so "erratic"—"such a nuisance"—when he was young. I know now that I was often a nuisance to him, but he never lost his patience, though he often feigned to. When he refused to take my various excitements seriously, he would chuckle and jest ironically;

but over and over again I encountered an indulgent sympathy with my unrestful thrashings about, even where, as I found out later and not from him, they were costing him not a little trouble. I have few memories of reproof or censure, though I know I often deserved them. For many needless vexations that he bore for me I often blame myself today. Any man can recall instances out of his own life where he caused annoyance to his elders; generally, I suppose, it is his father who has had to put up with it. With me, as I now see, Sumner was exceedingly patient and tolerant, suffering green youth with resignation.

He was very tender, as I have said, to children and to women. "Yes, babies are a bore sometimes; but I like 'em all. I enjoyed my own and I wish I could live all that over again." One day while we were walking he confided to me, rather quaintly: "Keller, I'm going to tell you something you mustn't say anything about for a while. By next January I am promised a grandson." When, after considerable persuasion, he had consented to don a priestly garb and baptize one of his grandchildren, it is reported that his voice broke as he remarked: "I never in my life saw anything so beautiful as that baby smiling up in my face." Of his grandson, he writes: "He preaches to his fingers and smiles at the bystanders." A colleague once confided to me that he thought Sumner called at his house purely to see the children. Protesting once against bringing a small child along to dinner at Sumner's house, I received, over the telephone, the blunt retort: "Then you needn't come yourself!" We all went. Seated at the table, he beamed on the youngster and, hidden from Mrs. Sumner by a large potted plant, slipped things upon the child's plate until his wife discovered him. "Graham! you *mustn't* feed such things to a little child!" she chided him, and he looked as nearly sheepish as was possible for him. Later he reverted to his delinquencies and, amidst some amusement, the maid was summoned to remove the barrier that hid his doings from the hostess.

As we strolled along Whitney Avenue, one day, his attention was attracted by a small, plump boy, incredibly soiled, who was sprawled on his stomach on the sidewalk, busily making marks in a smudgy notebook with a pencil-stump. Sumner was much amused.

1907

"Isn't that a dirty little boy?" he chuckled; then, coming closer, "Why, it's Tommy!"—a youngster he knew. He stopped. "What you doing, Tommy?" he asked, smiling broadly. The urchin replied importantly, not allowing himself to be diverted, that he was taking down all the numbers of all the automobiles that passed. "That's right!" Sumner encouraged, "that's the way to get 'em!" And he kept looking around and chuckling, as we went on. "He's beginning right, by collecting facts," he commented, "but he's getting pretty dirty doing it. I wonder what his mother will say. She's the one that'll have to clean him up."

"It's this way about children," he once remarked. "It's cumulative. The more you love them, the more you sacrifice; and the more you sacrifice, the more you love."

He used to speak with deep admiration of his mother-in-law. "She knew how to take care of babies, from the word *go*," he would begin, and then illustrate in detail. He had a deep respect for a certain baby food which, he said, had very likely saved the life of one of his children. He was all solicitude when two of our children had tonsillitis together, one winter, and would appear with some dainty—like custard frozen into rabbit form. He would never come in. "No, I might bring in the cold on them. This stuff is simple and can't hurt them, and cold things feel good to a hot throat. Jane [the Sumner cook] fixed it up herself. It can't hurt them at all."

I might continue at some length on this strain. There were many variations of it. I am moved to recur to the marvel of how that formidable face of his, that many a young man found forbidding or downright terrifying, never seemed to repel even young children. He always smiled broadly and helplessly at them. In any case, he had no difficulty in ingratiating himself. Astonishment is no name for the state of mind of some of us when we first encountered this side of Sumner.

He used to spend a long time in department store basements just before Christmas, selecting presents for children he knew, and once made an earnest though unsuccessful effort to get, through Mr. Camp, a real Yale football for my son—one that had been actually used by the players. For a number of years before his death, he regularly subscribed to *Saint Nicholas* for my children.

I AM urged, and am myself moved, to relate an incident that my family, even the youngest member of it, cannot forget. Though intimate, it is so utterly characteristic of the man. Upon Friday, December 24, 1909, occurred one of the walks and talks to which I so often refer. The day was rather warm. Sumner regretted more than a little that he was not to have his grandchild with him over Christmas, for the boy was slightly ailing. He seemed much disappointed. When I got home, my wife, having heard my report, wondered whether Mr. Sumner might not care to come to our family Christmas tree the next day, as a sort of substitute. I called him up and suggested it. "Yes, I'd like to," he replied promptly. "When does the function come off?" "At four o'clock." "Good. I'll be there, with thanks for being invited."

During that night it began to snow, and there was a sizable blizzard on, the next day. By afternoon the snow was deep and the sidewalks were not yet cleared, as the storm kept right on. As four o'clock approached, we agreed that Sumner would not come; but, on looking down the street, I saw him coming, toiling along through the deep snow a few yards at a time and then stopping to get his breath. When he got to the house, he was pretty well exhausted; but after we had relieved him of his wrappings and overshoes and got him into his chair, he began to brighten up, expand, and grin at the children who stood in a row before him, expectantly. To his immense amusement, the oldest, assuming spokesmanship, thanked him rather stiltedly for his beautiful presents—"just what we wanted." He began to talk to them, paying but brief heed to us, but winding up their mechanical toys for them and chattering along. There was an altercation between the youngest, about two and a half, and her brother. "That's right! Scold him!" Sumner encouraged her.

He sat there till after six, then rose: "Well, I must go home. Mrs. Sumner will think I'm lost. This has been fine." We helped him on with his things, and I said I would accompany him home. "No," he objected, "your place is right here." However, he gave in to my insistence upon seeing him to the trolley. He was very shaky and needed me to help him down the street. At the trolley, I wanted to go on with him, but he sternly refused: "*No*, Keller!

Your place is at home with your family. I'm all right." I helped him into the car and saw him move forward to pay his fare. I never saw him again.

I NEVER heard Sumner utter a harsh or depreciating word about a woman. He thought his own mother had died of appendicitis, unrecognized as such and called inflammation of the bowels. He told me once that he used, as a boy, to hate his stepmother; that she was pretty strict and severe, so that he and his brother thought they would like to kill her. "But," he would say, "that was all wrong. Nobody ever did more for me. She insisted on my going to college, and economized stringently so that I could." She was ungracious, he said, "but Lord knows she had enough to make her fussy. She was a good woman—one of the suffering righteous."

Concerning his family relations I can have little to relate—only that they were affectionate and indulgent in every way. He loved his wife, whom he often called "Liebchen," and admired her, so far as I could see, no less than when they both were young. He was always distressed at her slightest ailment or discomfort and elated at any evidence or prospect of returning health. She leaned always upon his knowledge and often asked me, after his death, whether I did not think "Graham" would have held such-and-such opinions—about Mr. Wilson, the War, and so on. She asked me what journal I thought most closely approached what he would have thought about such subjects, and subscribed to *The Nation*, then under the editorship, successively, of Lamont, More, and Fuller, as approaching her husband's point of view. She used to lament that Sumner had never been willing to put himself forward. They had once stayed in a summer hotel where Grover Cleveland was sojourning, but her husband had not tried even to meet him; had dismissed the suggestion with: "Oh, he doesn't want to be bothered with me."

He had always worked too hard, she said, and she had tried in vain to restrain him. An older colleague once told me that Sumner, having stayed in New Haven alone one summer and wrought incessantly, had extracted a promise "not to let on to Mrs. Sumner how much I've worked." In his later years, he moved downstairs from his attic study so that he and his wife could be together, she reading on the sofa and he working at his desk. They talked a good deal; "We give each other a lot of taffy about the boys."

On a certain evening, he told me, he was quite alone in the house, late at night, studying, when a telegram was delivered to him carrying news about a member of his family which he had been longing to hear. "I was so tickled that I stood right up there in the dark and shouted to the empty house: 'Whoop! Whoop!!' "

He was very courtly and considerate with women outside his family, admiring them especially for their motherhood and expressing commiseration for childlessness which, it seemed to me, he regarded as obviously a piece of pure misfortune.

In one of his brief autobiographical sketches, he states, concerning his father, that he was the wisest man he had ever known, and that as he himself had grown old, he had come to "hold with him, and not with the others." It is evident enough that the father's strictures on the tariff, doubtless heard all through childhood, whenever shoes had to be bought or clothing replaced, must have sunk deeply into the son's outfit of ideas. The elder Sumner, accustomed in earlier years to English conditions, apparently drew comparisons freely. Everything that Sumner used to say about the father revealed him as the prototype of the hardheadedness and stern fidelity to duty that characterized the son. Dr. Starr has presented a clear and unforgettable sketch of the father.

I AM able to report some details, set down immediately I returned, of a rambling conversation of Sunday, May 30, 1909. Sumner said he saw nothing any longer in economics—it was getting to be too metaphysical. I asked him how he got a positive, scientific trend out of his education in theology. He replied that he supposed it was in him; that, though "those Germans in Göttingen" had taught him much, he had learned it mainly from his father. He respected his father more every day since his death. He had been a man very hard to be taken in—would smile and say: "Wait and see."

He went on to say that he was pleased over his degree of LL.D., to be conferred the next month, especially as Mrs. Sumner seemed so delighted. He said he would rather have it from Yale than from any other college. He gave the impression of one who saw the world passing and did not care much anyway. He said he hadn't been to Commencement in twenty-five years. "I used to be sent off somewhere to hold entrance examinations; then I thought: 'If they can get along without me when I'm away from town, why not when I'm here?' So I stopped going to the exercises and worked at home as I did every other day. I haven't been since. I would have endured it if I had been needed."

His thought then turned to Oxford as it had appeared to him in his year there, long ago. He said that it was pleasant if one had $10,000 a year from his grandfather; then "one could be a gentleman and not worry over the other poor cusses who were working along." Oxford was quite apart from the world. When he came home and sat in the "tutors' box" in Old Chapel he felt that he had fallen in estate; but he knew that his future was "over here" and schooled his mind, in long Sunday walks, "to forget and not spoil my life by fussing."

He said he would be walking and think of some of his old views; suddenly realize that they were all gone—a blank. Gradually all of them went.

He talked a good deal about children—his grandchildren and my family. "I like them all—babies and all. Boys are a great care, but, darn it! they're worth it."

He said the Century Club was a fine club—good for a young man to belong to. He had tried to resign twice or so, as the dues were too high for him, using it as little as he did. Now they had fixed it so one could remain on the list and not pay—or come; but this had led him to keep away. They wouldn't let him resign. He got there only once or twice a year. It was a good club to belong to if one could afford it.

SUMNER used occasionally to speak with affection of his brother. "He and I," he would say, "used to wake up Sunday mornings and be very cheerful until we realized what day it was; and then we condoled with each other." I have had the honor of knowing Sumner's half-sister, younger than he by many years, and the privilege of hearing from her many instances of his love and loyalty to those who were close to him. To all of these he was constantly and tenderly devoted. An outsider like myself could perceive this clearly enough from what he happened to observe. I am tempted to enlarge upon this topic, in view of the prevalent misconception of Sumner as a hard, cold man; but I have gone as far as anyone outside his family should. He could be very rough to men; he was never so to any woman or child; and to his family he was all that a husband, father, and brother could be. I suppose that the only criticism that could have been lodged against him by his family was his absorption in work; I judge that his hours often ran into figures that he strove to keep to himself; they might have wished that his loyalty to his position in the University and his intellectual curiosity had been less demanding.

As a matter of fact, when it came to his vital resources, he lived prodigally, even dangerously. His theory of life seemed to be to spend strength, not to hoard or even to conserve it. He got into the way, apparently, of believing himself strong enough not to require cautionary or precautionary measures. He had a powerful body and a rugged constitution, or he could not have done all he did, in the way he did it, and yet have lived almost to three score and ten. I have said that, until he was compelled, he took no regular exercise or other relaxation. He was also rather reckless as to diet. I recall dining at his house soon after I became a student in the graduate school. There was some kind of fruit for dessert and a pitcher of thick cream was passed. When I declined it, Sumner said: "I'm afraid you don't appreciate the good things of life" and helped himself liberally. He used to say to me sometimes, as we returned from a Sunday afternoon walk: "You'd better stay and have supper. We always have a good one, creamed chicken or the like, Sunday nights. We got into the habit of enticing the boys home Sundays by having an extra good meal." He was a vigorous trencherman, though he never attained to even the beginnings of obesity; it seemed to take a good deal of fuel to keep up his tremendous head of steam.

He used alcoholic drinks sparingly. Once he told someone that, after he was sixty, he thought he would take a little whiskey every day. A friend, hearing of this, sent him a case of fine Scotch and Rye. Later he remarked that he hadn't used much of it—"just a little, on grapefruit, now and then." But he was a lusty drinker of tea, emptying one cup after another all through a dinner.

Concerning his use of tobacco the tale is an incredible one. His wife, remonstrating a little with the present writer on the score of smoking too much, was seconded by her husband. "Did you never smoke?" I asked him. He looked at his wife and smiled a little sheepishly, as she replied that he used to light one cigar from another, all day long. "Yes," he said, "I used to smoke twenty fifteen-cent cigars a day, and if I'd kept it up I'd have been under the sod long ago." When, on a later occasion, the same subject came up, I asked: "When did you stop?" "September the eighth, 1879," he replied, to my amazement. "Do you mean to say you quit that day, short off?" "Yes," he replied, "I've never smoked since. I was figuring up my monthly accounts and noticed, to my astonishment and disgust, that my tobacco bill was equal to that for certain prime necessities of life. 'This is hoggish!' I said to myself, and I quit then and there. There were a few cigars in the box yet. I threw them away." "But," I exclaimed, "wasn't it pretty hard?" "Yes, till I got around the corner. I had to give up all my clubs, for I couldn't stand it to see and smell the rest smoking. I like the smell now and always keep a box of cigars around for my guests, but they don't tempt me any more." "Wouldn't it have been better," I suggested, "to have smoked less and not cut yourself out of all your associations?" "It might have been. Very likely. But that's what I did; and it's lucky for me that I swore off."

Much later I heard one of his students of the seventies remark how Sumner used sometimes in class to stick his thumbs in the armholes of his vest, thus inadvertently revealing two serried ranks of cigars in his upper vest pockets. This was not a little diverting to his class, especially as Sumner had not yet, despite Herculean efforts, managed to shake off the "Rev." that preceded his name in the catalogue. All "Rev.'s," in those days, were prime exhibits for a college. I do not suppose that this unconsciously revealed evidence of human weakness ever hurt him much in the eyes of youth.

One time he remarked to me that smoking was not only probably bad for health, but so very expensive. "Yes," said I, "if you smoke the kind of tobacco you did." "Well," he asked, "what do your cigars cost you?" I told him. "Oh, well, then," he replied, "they're not tobacco at all. Probably fern-leaf. I guess they won't hurt you much."

WHEN he got going in his work, Sumner hated to be interrupted as much as some of us, very likely under less pressure from within, like to be. Under such circumstances, he was wont to be pretty gruff. One day, reports his former secretary, when they were laboring in his attic-study which, with its dormer windows, was a little dark anyway, a heavy thunderstorm came up, rendering further work by daylight impossible. "It doesn't seem as if this were necessary," grumbled Sumner. "We'd better stop awhile." One can readily imagine his state of mind when, at length, he was forbidden to work at all for a couple of years. Apparently he could not understand how such a thing could have happened to him. And there was so much to do. He told me that he used to work from eight to twelve hours a day; but I have always suspected that, if the whole truth were known, he had often sneaked in much more than this, at the expense of sleep.

Professor Henry C. Emery used to recount, apropos of Sumner's self-seclusion, his first meeting with Sumner something as follows: "When I was appointed at Yale and came down to New Haven, I saw Sumner now and then but made no effort to call on him. Presently my father [Chief Justice Emery of the Supreme Court of Maine] came to visit me. The first thing he asked me was: 'Well, what do you think of Sumner?' I said I hadn't met him yet. 'What!' exclaimed my father, 'not met Sumner! What have you been doing, then?' I told him the old boy wasn't well and was said to be pretty grouchy—anyway, he didn't want to see me for anything. 'While I'm here,' said my father emphatically, 'you will take me to call on him.' I remonstrated, saying that Sumner didn't want to see anybody, but my father replied that if I wouldn't take him he'd go alone. So I called Sumner up and asked him—it was Wednesday morning—for an appointment. He was gruff. 'Can't see you today. Busy,' he growled. 'How about tomorrow?' I persisted. 'No! Busy!' I kept at it. 'Then could we come Friday?' There was a long pause, while he was evidently thinking how he could get out of it, then: 'Come today. At two,' he snapped and hung up. We went out there, and I was pretty nervous. Father wasn't. Sumner himself came to the door; I couldn't think of anything to say, but Father was all set. He stepped forward and held out his hand: 'Professor Sumner, I'm the Forgotten Man.' Sumner was very nice, and those two old boys went into the parlor and, paying no attention at all to me, had a grand time knocking everything that had happened since the Civil War."

Sumner seems never to have been halted by the eye-strain that so frequently puts the brakes upon over-exertion. Apparently his eyes had about the same sensitiveness to weariness as a camera. I do not know when he began to use glasses for close work, but a mental picture of him never includes them.

In his summers, at Seal Harbor, he evidently did a great deal of walking. "When I was walking around up at Mount Desert," was the preface to a good many anecdotes. "There's an island up there, way out in the ocean," he once recounted. "On clear days you can just see it. One day, when I was walking with Whitney, that island was just a bright, single point 'way out there. Whitney looked at it awhile and then said: 'Bill, what a place for a philosopher to live! He wouldn't have to be bothered by any practical facts of life at all!' "

On one of our walks, we climbed part way up East Rock. Sumner, a little breathless, slumped rather heavily against one of the round wooden railings that stretched between heavy posts along the edge of a drop, almost sheer, of fifteen or twenty feet. As I was about to lean back against it, a yard or two from him, the railing —a tree-trunk four inches or so in diameter—started to give way behind me. Fortunately I was able to whirl about and seize it while it was still holding to the post the other side of Sumner. As I pulled it and him back, he regained his equilibrium just as it gave way altogether and crashed down. He stepped in silence to the edge of the steep declivity—a wall of rock built up to level the road—and viewed the situation for a moment in silence. "Pretty close shave," he commented, judicially. "We'd better report the break to the Park officials. Somebody might get a bad fall. I guess it would have killed me." As if that contingency were of little moment, he resumed what he had been saying and did not return to the incident. It was very startling. I have thought of it often since, imagining what might have happened if, in spite of his feebleness at the time, he had not been so quick to regain his balance.

Sumner used to say that he liked to see the cold weather come, for it always stimulated him so that he could work better. When he was enervated his head would begin to bother him and he would be wakeful. There were noises in his head then, he said, more like crickets than anything else and very annoying.

He hated to shave, and commended a colleague who was growing a beard. "I raised one once, when I was in Europe," he remarked. "It wasn't a very good one, and when I came home, Mrs. Sumner made me cut it off." These last words were rather mournful. I think he begrudged the time it took to shave and, after the advent of the safety razor, he hated to clean the instrument after using. He used to cut himself pretty often, even with the safety. I think he was naturally a little clumsy with his hands, as well as always impatient of such tasks.

It is evident from much that precedes that though he spent himself freely—even extravagantly, often rather clumsily—he was always trying to make his efforts go as far as possible. Just what a "single-track mind" may now mean, it is hard to say; but Sumner was, in all his variety, single-minded. He had been intrusted with the development of political and social science (thus reads the title of his professorship), and he set his life, without reservation or qualification, to that task. I could revert voluminously to his sense of duty, which has often impressed me as his salient characteristic; but if that quality does not emerge in stark outline from these reminiscences as a whole, then I shall have conveyed no net impressions.

FROM time to time in these recollections has appeared the question of Sumner's relation to religion. For the moment, let us assume that "religion" means identification with the church and with some creed. I once heard Sumner regret that he had not gone into the law; nevertheless, he told his class, at their fortieth reunion, that teaching had been best for him. "The life of a professor is so simple and monotonous that I know of no other 'history' of it that is possible, than what I have just written. No other life could have been so well suited to my taste as this." When he graduated, in 1863, I suppose he naturally expected, like most scholarly men of that time, to go into some profession. But certainly there is no intimation that, however much he admired the great doctor or natural scientist, he ever contemplated entering either of these vocations. There is, so far as I know, no existing evidence indicative of the youthful Sumner's state of mind, as predisposing him for the ministry, except his early sermons, many of which are preserved. They witness to a far more religious or even pious disposition than those who knew Sumner later have credited him with. These sermons are not at all evangelistic, but their phraseology at least is religious. They inculcate the ethical rather than the mystical or theological; still, there is an element there that had no counterpart in the Sumner I knew.

In this connection, I recall a significant remark that he once made to me. "I have never discarded beliefs deliberately. I left them in the drawer, and, after a while, when I opened it, there was nothing there at all." Again, speaking of a friend who, feeling himself emancipated from former beliefs, thought he ought to try to disillusion and instruct others: "I said to him: 'Now you've got rid of all that, why don't you get the enjoyment of it? Let 'em think what they will and don't mar your own serenity.' "

What happened to Sumner, I take it, is that gradually, as his words indicate, he grew out of one phase into another, without any special heartburning or wrench. He repeated to me several times what I have just set down—that he had not consciously, as a result of skepticism, rejected any doctrine, but would come back to some question of aforetime, and behold! it was all gone. He used to laugh at himself for his presentiment, the first time he traveled by rail on Sunday, in Europe, "that there would be a smash-up." He said that he thought religion (creeds) was collapsing and tumbling down on all sides, and that the younger generation might live to see its end. It has been stated by his parishioners that his sermons gradually took on an economic tinge, as, indeed, they seem to do to one who now reads them; and that he himself said that he had told his hearers all he had to say about right living and did not wish to repeat himself.

The wildest judgment I ever heard of upon Sumner was from an older man, a professor of art, who said he knew Sumner well—remembered when he came to Yale to teach; that he himself had never been a disciple of Sumner, who seemed to him "utterly oblivious to the influence of the spiritual."

The fact is that Sumner was a great-hearted, generous soul; it was because the woes of men hurt him as they did that he was so inexorably truthful in stating the facts about life at their hardest and also so ruthless in his denunciation of predatory shammers and oily hypocrites.

This is about all the background I can supply or infer. He simply did not talk much about religion, in classes or out, except to develop its evolution after the manner of Spencer, Tylor, Lippert, and Frazer. Most of my impressions about his private attitude while I knew him are negative and inferential. Before I come to them, it is in order, perhaps, to speculate a little on that matter of Sumner's continued connection with the (Episcopal) church, which was maintained up to his death. He needs no defense; and if he did, I should be the last to offer one. But there has always been some curiosity on this score, which is legitimate enough.

"If so candid and fearless a man no longer believed," some have puzzled, "why did he not get out of the ministry, at any rate, if not out of the church?" This question never rose in my association with Sumner, and so I cannot answer it; but the following considerations seem to me to have their bearing upon the matter. In youth, Sumner was profoundly influenced by the Göttingen theologians, against whom he had been warned by obscurantists here for whom he had little respect. I do not know that these Germans were later repudiated by the church; it is my impression that liberals have long ago accepted them. Again, the church to which Sumner belonged has been pretty tolerant in spirit. It has not anathematized dancing, card-playing, and the theater. It has not been so painfully holy. I do not see that he must have been forced out of it by conscience, as he might well have been from more primitive and neurotic, or more rigidly dogmatic, sects. It is quite possible, too, that Sumner was led to avoid any open rupture that did not seem to him imperative, by consideration for the feelings of those who were near and dear to him. I think he would cheerfully have stretched himself on the rack or risked the lowest Inferno, at any time, to spare them pain.

Though I do not think it would have been possible for him to have kept silence where he felt that reticence conveyed a false impression, he was certainly reticent about religion, as he was about all other personal matters. I have mentioned the fact that he never entered into religious controversy, so far as I know, at any rate, and that his peaceableness in that range contrasted strongly with his readiness to become embroiled in economic or political battles. At any rate, he was not nearly as outspoken on religious matters as was Spencer, and his justification of himself for presuming to use Spencer's books against the opposition of Dr. Porter does not really join issue on religious grounds at all, unless championship of academic freedom can be so construed. Further, in his courses—undergraduate or graduate—he did not develop the implications of certain phenomena in the evolution of religion—say, the parallels between different messiahs and the attending mythology—to nearly the degree found in the writings of others, notably Frazer, with whose books he was intimately familiar.

If I had to label Sumner with a current label, I should say that he was an agnostic. Perhaps if this were assumed to be the case, the original query might shift into another form: Is it possible for an agnostic to be religious, in the definite sense we have agreed, for the moment, to accept?

I do not know enough about the church Sumner was affiliated with to expound on this issue; but I have the acquaintance of several men whom I respect very highly, clergymen in that church who, knowing Sumner very well, apparently saw nothing amiss in his continued connection with their organization. I cannot believe that Sumner credited the Virgin Birth, the miracles, or any other of those mysteries which have been brought into question by liberal clergymen of several denominations in recent years. I suppose there must have been in Sumner's day a good many honest church members, clerical and lay, who had long ceased to believe in such dogmas without feeling it necessary to seek exit from the church. I take it that persons of that sort have regarded traditional dogmas and creeds as rather harmless survivals, and a perception of this fact as nothing worth making a great stir about. I have always regarded Sumner as belonging to that class of persons. I think it is easy to see why he wanted the "Rev." left off his name, but not at all obvious that he should have felt it incumbent upon him to renounce the church, or even the priesthood.

In short, on the small evidence concerning Sumner's inner life possessed by me or by anyone I know about, I cannot see any default of candor or conscience in what he chose to do, or not to do.

If we should widen the term "religious" somewhat, as is common enough today, to mean "spiritually-minded," Sumner was all of that. I suppose that if "religious" means "belonging to a church," Sumner was religious; if, on the other hand, it means literal acceptance of a creed, he was not religious. If "religious" means, as it does to not a few nowadays, simply "good" or "ethical," he was religious. If it means that one is "spiritually-minded"—aware of the inexplicable mystery that bounds our small sphere of knowledge and sensitive to the presence of endless, impersonal power in the universe—then Sumner, like any other profound student of nature or of society who possesses insight, was religious. But what is the use in playing with terms? We know something of what Sumner was—a big, generous, incorruptible human soul. What matter whether he is labeled this or that?

I think he was a little afraid—and he has not been alone in that fear—that he might, in the weakening of his faculties by age or illness, revert to a seeming re-acceptation of outlived views. "We don't know what we'll think or say when we get old and weak and lose our grip. I hope I don't live long enough to make a fool of myself."

I never heard him say anything about a belief or non-belief in a future life. I am told that, in an interval of lucidity not long before his death, he spoke to one of the family of "the Dark River into which he felt he was going. 'Oh,' I said, 'Love doesn't stop there; love goes right on forever.' He said: 'We think so'; then, having paused a moment: 'We hope so.'

"He accepted the disability of the last year of his life silently, with a graciousness moving to see. It is impossible to describe the charming courtesy with which he said, 'I am so glad to have a daughter,' as one helped him with his overcoat or with buttoning a glove. He repeatedly enjoined his sons: 'Take care of your Mother; be sure and take care of her.' A quality shown through the clouded days of his long illness that impressed all who saw him. Far beyond fortitude and acceptance, in this man of massive strength, was revealed a delicacy, a gentleness, a constant consideration for others, profoundly touching and revealing. A spiritual beauty glowed through broken human conditions, most renewing to those who perceived it—to those to whom he gave this absurd and beautiful worship of his."

Sumner spoke of death with no evidence of concern. Having heard, during the first days of January, 1908, that he was confined to his house, I went in to see him. He was sitting in his big chair, with dressing gown on, as in the frontispiece of *The Forgotten Man and Other Essays*, here reproduced, but with his right hand in a sling. It looked swollen and inert to me, and I thought, with a sinking of heart, that I recognized the marks of paralysis. "Well, I just heard you had had an accident," I said, dissembling. "What is it? Have you had a fall?" "No, no!" he replied, cheerfully, "it's lots more interesting than that. The doctors are having a good time over me." He paused and resumed, in a low voice and first looking to see that no one was within ear-shot: "Keller, it's the home stretch."

He cautioned me first to say nothing about the real nature of his malady: "Mrs. Sumner is naïve as a girl about such things, but she has a horror of paralysis. She thinks there's something the matter with the circulation—and there is, too, only she needn't know just what." Then he told me he was glad I had come in, for he wanted to get everything fixed up betimes. He spoke of his coming retirement and talked of what he had planned for the department. I hope I may be pardoned for repeating one of his remarks, which will remain in my memory while I live: "I don't often say much about such matters," he began, "but I want you to know that since you have been with me *I've—been—happy.*" He went on to mention some of the annoyances he had suffered in years past, which he said had been wholly spared him since Bishop and I had been with him. Everything had gone smoothly, he declared, and in a wholly friendly and enjoyable way. "Anyway, I want you to know this now, when the end is not far away."

Several weeks later he handed me a full accounting of some small funds—a few hundred dollars—which he had been hoarding and administrating for the department. He had "begged" this small sum at some time in the past, from "Bill Whitney" and "Dim" (Henry Dimock), and had been doling it out, with careful scrutiny of every item. The accounting he handed over to me was on a large sheet of paper, painfully written with his left hand. He apologized for its occasional blots and illegibility. "It's pretty bad, but I guess you can read it. It's accurate, anyway." He sighed. "It's taken me several days' work to make it out." "Oh, Lord!" I broke out, "how am I going to take up this work after you!" "Nonsense!" he retorted. "You'll do it a lot better. You'll read all the books, and there'll be more of them, and better; and you'll have a lot more to give the classes. Nobody is indispensable—ever." And he went on to tell me about how he had fumbled, got on the wrong track, had had to do work all over again, and had been forced to abandon the results of much labor upon aspects of society's life that had originally been on his list but which, with the growth of the subject, he had been forced to abandon. "I had planned books on all these subjects," he said, "but they're all dead babies. I've set up tombstones over them all. If I had it to do all over again, I would limit myself more. But you couldn't tell, back there, what the best lines of study were. It only came out after you'd tried. I spent a lot of time finding out what not to do." Which recalls one of his pregnant utterances: "You've got to find out where it isn't before you find out where it is."

The conversation I have recorded took place two years or more before his death. He cleared up the whole situation at that time, or shortly after, and never, to my remembrance, resumed the subject. It had been attended to, and was set aside. The passages between us touching upon my continuance and completion of *The Science of Society* are detailed, for those who may be interested, in the preface to that book. I repeat here only that magnanimous injunction of his, to make all changes I saw fit, and not to let "the dead hand" shadow the work.

Only incidentally did his approaching retirement come up again. He seemed to assume that I now understood about everything; he always refrained from offering advice, in any case, unless it was solicited. Least of all, I repeat, did he exhibit any concern about oncoming death; he was, like Darwin, again, "not in the least afraid to die." He calmly stated, now and then, that he was "losing his grip" over his classes, but never seemed to bewail the fact. The impression was as of one who had lived his life and was not at all unwilling to lay it down. Indeed, I think he was more cheerful during his last two years than before; for one thing, his wife's health was much better, as he used recurrently to tell me, always very complacently. She seems to me always to have been the supreme interest of his life.

He said that he liked his retirement, instancing late breakfasts as one of its chief attractions. He had had, for years and years, an eight-thirty class, at which he planned to arrive at eight-fifteen, and it was a relief, he said, "not to have to be there—in fact, I don't have to be anywhere at any time." He and his wife spent many long hours together, to their deep satisfaction.

"I have lived," said Sumner, "through the best period of this country's history. The next generations are going to see war and social calamities. I am glad I don't have to live on into them."

In brief, there was nothing sad or melancholy about his latter years, so far as I could see. Certainly whatever religion, or non-religion, or life-philosophy he had, it sustained him enviably, with the shadow of the end always impending. If one prays for dignity in his passing, he could well envy Sumner's state of mind during those last months.

The 1909 Christmas meeting of the American Sociological Society was to be held in New York. Sumner was President that year. He meant to take the 9.35 train and, as usual and despite the heavy snowfall, had been on time and had been seen to board the first section, which had pulled out already when I arrived. I was relieved to hear that he had been seen to embark and had seemed all right. We arrived late in New York and went immediately to the Metropolitan Building, where the sessions were to be held. Sumner's address was scheduled for twelve, noon. As the hour approached and he failed to appear, I grew uneasy, for he was never late. We telephoned the Murray Hill Hotel, where he always stayed, and found that he had had a stroke there and was not expected to live. Emery, Bishop, and I hurried up town, to do what we could; but his family had arrived and there was nothing to do. I had no heart for the meetings and went home.

Sumner had dragged himself off that morning, ill and weak but as determined as ever, with his manuscript carefully prepared, typewritten and corrected, in his valise. No remonstrances could have stopped him. Nothing could have been more in keeping with his life than this episode, where he struggled up to the battle-line, mortally exhausted, but armed and resolute. "How characteristic of Sumner!" was the common remark at the tidings of his fall.

I SHOULD call Sumner a realistic, single-minded truth-seeker, who suspended all judgment upon unverifiable matters of a supernatural order, and who lived a life of singular purity, incorruptible honor, and sympathetic helpfulness. He was a good man. He was of the same type as Darwin, Lincoln, and the rest of that intrepidly honest, magnanimous band, gifted with uncommon insight into the secrets of human life, to whom we all, as Sumner said of Darwin, "owe so much." "We must never forget all that Mr. Darwin has done for us." Believing, as some of us do, in the eventual recognition of Sumner as a much greater figure than he has been, or now is, we expect that much the same will sometime be said of Sumner that he said of Darwin. We must remember all that Mr. Sumner did for us. Many of us require no such injunction; we could not forget if we would; our sense of obligation and reverence is too profound. We want to know, and to recall, all we can of a great soul's earthly pilgrimage. He was not alone an opener of minds; he was also a strengthener of hearts.